Planning for Overlord – Sword Beach and the British Airl

The first real plan for the Normandy landings was known as the COSSAC plan, named for the Chief-of-Staff Supreme Allied Commander staff under Lieutenant General Sir Frederick Morgan. This plan was devised in late 1943, but was disliked by Eisenhower and Montgomery. The American commander objected to the plan because it called for a narrow-front landing by a mere three divisions with only two more divisions as floating reserve, failed to allow for a rapid build-up in the beach-head area, and made no provision for the capture of Cherbourg at the head of the Cotentin peninsula. Eisenhower was adamant that the early seizure of a major port was essential for the assured delivery of the follow-on forces and the supplies that were essential for the beach-head to be expanded.

Montgomery objected to the COSSAC plan on the ground that it provided too narrow a landing, especially as by D + 12 some 12 divisions were scheduled to land over the same beaches, this figure increasing to 24 divisions by D + 24. In these circumstances Montgomery anticipated that the beach areas would become jammed, throwing Allied operations completely out of gear and providing ideal targets for German air (and missile) attack. Montgomery went one step further than criticizing the COSSAC plan and suggested his own ideal concept, in which a broad-front landing would be made after the completion of an Allied air offensive to eliminate German air units in the area. Montgomery thus advocated that the Anglo-Canadian and US armies should each have their own group of landing beaches, each beach being used for a single corps (both assault divisions and follow-up divisions) and sufficiently separated from other beaches so that each corps would have freedom of tactical action in developing its beach-head before the entire army group moved rapidly to secure at least two major ports or groups of smaller ports.

Eisenhower realized the value of his subordinate's point of view, and modifications were worked into the basic COSSAC scheme. The Overlord plan therefore added two more beaches, in the form of Sword Beach at Lion-sur-Mer on the left and Utah Beach at Les Dunes de Varreville on the right, so that five divisions could be landed in the first assault wave, joining the three airborne divisions already landed, against the four German divisions of General Erich Marcks' LXXXIV Corps of which only two be fully engaged. Montgomery's revisions meant in effect that eight Allied divisions would be attacking three German divisions, offering better chances of success than the COSSAC scheme, which pitched three Allied divisions against two German divisions. Other advantages of the revised plan were the availability of seven Allied divisions to follow the assault wave, and the fact that the westward

The build-up in the southern UK for Overlord demanded the assembly of the assault divisions within easy reach of southern embarkation ports virtually opposite Normandy, while the areas for the assault corps' follow-up divisions were slightly farther north but still within short distance of the selected embarkation ports. The follow-up corps' divisions were located farther inland or, in the case of one British and one Canadian corps, in the south-east of England where their presence would suggest to the Germans the likelihood of an invasion across the Straits of Dover into the Pas-de-Calais.

extension of the assault area to include Utah Beach on the eastern side of the Cotentin peninsula allowed for a rapid development north through the peninsula to Cherbourg even if the Germans managed to hold the line of the River Vire to prevent the other Allied forces sweeping west into the Cotentin peninsula.

There can be little doubt that the revised plan was considerably superior to its predecessor, but its development meant that Overlord had to be postponed from early May to early June 1944, the precise date of the invasion being determined by the need for a full or almost full moon for the nocturnal delivery of the three airborne divisions, coinciding with low water shortly after dawn so that the Allied air forces could provide tactical air support for the airborne forces and deal with any last German gun emplacements before the assault proper began at low water. This last was necessary as Rommel had developed the number and capability of the German obstacles and mines on the beaches, and these would only be exposed at low water. These considerations indicated an invasion between 5 and 7 June 1944, weather permitting, so detailed plans were worked out by Montgomery's 21st Army Group staff and troops began to move up towards their loading areas for Operation Neptune, the naval operation that would take them to Normandy.

The Allied assault forces were gathered in the south of the UK for their embarkation. On the eastern edge of the Allied assault were the Sword and Juno Beaches to be attacked by the two forward divisions of the British Second Army's I Corps, the two infantry divisions' left flank being protected by the previous landing of the British 6th Airborne Division.

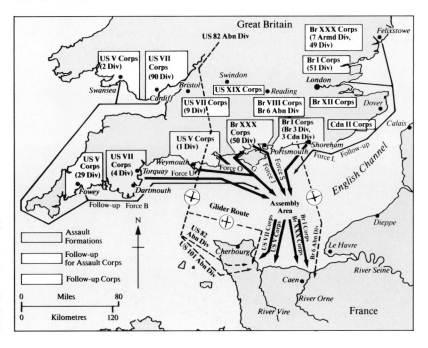

British Second Army

The main assault formation for the eastern part of the Overlord landings was the British Second Army, commanded by Lieutenant General Sir Miles Dempsey, who was 48 years old and had established his reputation as the commander of the British XIII Corps in General Sir Bernard Montgomery's British Eighth Army in the conquest of Sicily during July and August of the previous year. Dempsey was now known as a determined but steady commander who was appreciated by his superiors as well as admired by his subordinates, and among his most important attributes was taking the trouble to get to know his troops so that his battle plan exploited their strengths on the one hand but took account of their limitations on the other hand.

In Operation Overlord, the British Second Army was to land three infantry divisions, each supported by its own specially trained armoured brigade, on separate Sword, Juno and Gold Beaches as the leading elements of the army's left-hand British I Corps and right-hand British XXX Corps. The objective of these three landings, together with that of the US V Corps on Omaha Beach, was by the end of the first day to secure a consolidated beach-head some five to six miles deep between Cabourg at the mouth of the River Dives and Isigny at the mouth of the River Vire on the eastern and western ends of the lodgement respectively: this lodgement was also to include the cities of Bayeux and Caen, and provide the area for the arrival and deployment of additional divisions so that the Allied lodgement could be expanded to the south. The flanks of the initial assault area (including the separate area in the Cotentin peninsula earmarked for the US VII Corps) were to be secured by airborne operations, that on the British eastern flank being entrusted to the British 6th Airborne Division.

The arrival of these flank guards was to be the first element of the Allied operation, so it was only after the British 6th Airborne Division had landed from the air that the three infantry divisions of the seaborne assault forces were to arrive in three echelons. In the assault wave the British I Corps was to land, on Sword Beach, Major General T.G. Rennie's British 3rd Infantry Division (gathered in southern Sussex and embarked at Shoreham) supported by the British 27th Armoured Brigade. Specialized armour support for these British formations was provided by the 'funnies' of Major General Sir Percy Hobart's British 79th Armoured Division, which was under army group command with two of its brigades divided into regimental units for allocation to subordinate formations. In the follow-up wave Sword Beach was to witness the arrival of the British I Corps' other organic division.

Lieutenant General Sir Miles Dempsey's quiet but forceful character was a source of confidence.

BRITISH 79th ARMOURED DIVISION
(Major General Sir Percy C.S. Hobart)

30th ARMOURED BRIGADE
(Brigadier N.W. Duncan)
22nd Dragoons
2nd County of London Yeomanry (Westminster Dragoons)
141st Regiment Royal Armoured Corps
1st Lothians and Border Horse [arrived after D-Day]

1st ASSAULT BRIGADE & ASSAULT PARK SQUADRON, ROYAL ENGINEERS
(Brigadier G.L. Watkinson)
5th and 6th Assault Regiments, Royal Engineers
42nd Assault Regiment, Royal Engineers [arrived after D-Day]

1st TANK BRIGADE [arrived after D-Day]
(Brigadier T.R. Price)
31st TANK BRIGADE [arrived after D-Day]
(Brigadier G.S. Knight)

BRITISH SECOND ARMY
(Lieutenant General Sir Miles Dempsey)

BRITISH I CORPS
(Lieutenant General J.T. Crocker)

3rd Infantry Division
(Major General G.T. Rennie)

6th Airborne Division
(Major General R.N. Gale)

51st (Highland) Infantry Division
[landed from evening of D-Day]
(Major General D.C. Bullen-Smith)

Canadian 3rd Infantry Division
[landed on 'Juno' Beach]
(Major General R.F.L. Keller)

BRITISH XXX CORPS
(Lieutenant General G.C. Bucknall)

50th (Northumbrian) Infantry Division
[landed on 'Gold' Beach]
(Major General D.A.H. Graham)

49th (West Riding) Infantry Division
[landed on 'Gold' Beach after D-Day]
(Major General E.H. Barker)

7th Armoured Division
[landed on 'Gold' Beach after D-Day]
(Major General G.W.E.J. Erskine)

British I Corps

Led by Lieutenant General J.T. Crocker, who had commanded the British IX Corps in the final stages of the North African campaign during 1943 until he was wounded, the British I Corps had one of the most difficult and daunting tasks facing any Allied formation embroiled in Operation Overlord, namely separate landings on two beaches linked by the 4th Special Service Brigade, followed by an eight-mile advance to the south with the strategically important object of taking both Caen and the airfield just to its west at Carpiquet after linking up with the units holding the airhead seized to the east of the River Orne by the British 6th Airborne Division.

The difficulties facing the British I Corps in the execution of its task were compounded by the fact that in its sector, to the east and south of Caen, was the only armoured formation available to the opposition in this area, namely the highly celebrated 21st Panzer Division commanded by Generalleutnant Edgar Feuchtinger and currently held in army group reserve by Generalfeldmarschal Erwin Rommel's Army Group 'B'. It was believed that the 21st Panzer Division would not be committed until the true axes of the British I Corps' attacks became clear, so the primary foe to be faced by the British assault units in the opening phases of the landing was the forward regiment of the German Seventh Army's LXXXIV Corps commanded by General Erich Marcks. This regiment was the 736th Grenadier Regiment, commanded by Oberst Hafner, of Generalleutnant Wilhelm Richter's German 716th Infantry Division, which had been mustered in April 1941 from older personnel, and in the following month

had been allocated to the Caen sector in Normandy. Here the division had remained ever since, and taken a major part in preparing the area's defences.

The assault area allocated to the British 3rd Infantry Division was the easternmost of the landing areas, and was separated from the assault area of the Canadian 3rd Infantry Division, its partner in the British I Corps, by a gap of three miles: the most eastern point allocated to the Canadian 3rd Infantry Division was St. Aubin-sur-Mer, while the most western point entrusted to the British 3rd Infantry Division was Lion-sur-Mer. Lion-sur-Mer was a small watering place, and the assault area extended some two and one-half miles east from this spot to the small port of Ouistreham on the western side of the River Orne's estuary. The coast between Lion-sur-Mer and Ouistreham is flat, and a coastal road fringed by houses connected the two towns. Ouistreham and Lion-sur-Mer had each been turned into a major fortified strongpoint. So too had la Brèche, a village about midway between the two larger towns. These three spots were the core of the German's forward defence, and each strongpoint comprised guns in reinforced concrete casemates, mortar and machine gun positions, and wire-protected entrenchments for the infantry. And before they could tackle these land defences, the British assault units had first to overcome the beach defences, which comprised an outer band of underwater obstacles designed to rip the bottoms out of landing craft, a central band of mined posts, and then an inner band of steel 'hedgehog' obstacles.

Lieutenant General J.T. Crocker was one of those officers whose performance in the North African and Sicilian campaigns had attracted the attention of Montgomery.

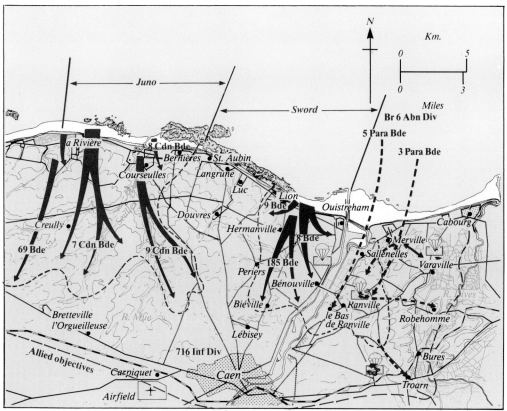

The single most important objective for the Allies on D-Day was the city of Caen, which fell into the area of the British I Corps. Besides being the primary road, rail and waterway junction of Normandy, the city also had an important airfield at Carpiquet, and its capture by I Corps would greatly hamper the lateral movement of German forces as well as facilitate the development of the British half of the allied lodgement. Unfortunately for the Allies, the city lay just beyond the movement range of formations that had been schooled in methodical rather than enterprising advance.

British 3rd Infantry Division

The formation entrusted with the assault landing on Sword Beach was the British 3rd Infantry Division commanded by Major General T.G. Rennie. The Division was to land on a narrow one-brigade front over Queen assault beach to the west of la Brèche, with No.4 Commando of the 1st Special Service Brigade coming ashore on the Roger assault beach to the east of la Brèche toward Ouistreham. The assault of the British 3rd Infantry Division was to be made by the 8th Infantry Brigade, with the 185th and 9th Infantry Brigades following in that order: the object of the one-brigade front was the creation of a concentrated mass that could punch through the German defences without delay to reach and take Caen, the major road, rail and waterway nexus of the region, and to link up with the lightly-equipped units of the British 6th Airborne Division holding the British 3rd Infantry Division's eastern flank along the River Orne.

The British 3rd Infantry Division was a formation with some pedigree, for it was already in existence at the beginning of World War II as a field formation of the regular army, remained an infantry division until June 1942, when it was turned into a mixed division by the replacement of one infantry brigade by one tank brigade, but then reverted to an infantry organization during April 1943. The British 3rd Infantry Division was commanded by Major General B.L. Montgomery at the start of hostilities, when its three components were the 7th Infantry Brigade (Guards), the 8th Infantry Brigade and the 9th Infantry Brigade. It was with these brigades that the division moved to France from 30 September 1939 as a component of the British Expeditionary Force's British II Corps, finally seeing action on the Ypres and Comines Canal sector between 26 and 28 May before falling back to Dunkirk, from which it was evacuated to England on 31 May 1940.

The division remained in the UK from 1 June 1940 until its departure for Operation Overlord on 4 June 1944, and in this four-year period came under successive control of the GHQ Home Forces and British XI Corps before finally becoming part of the British I Corps on 23 March 1943. During this period divisional command was exercised by Brigadier K.A.N. Anderson (acting) from 30 May 1940, Montgomery from 3 June 1940, Brigadier J.A.C. Whitaker (acting) from 22 July 1940, Major General J.A.H. Gammell from 25 July 1940, Major General E.C. Hayes from 20 November 1941, and Major General W.H.C. Ramsden from 15 December 1942.

Major General T.G. Rennie became divisional commander on 12 December 1943, and led the formation in the Normandy landing until 13 June 1944, when he was wounded and replaced by Brigadier E.E.E. Cass (acting) until 23 June 1944 and the arrival of of Major General L.G. Whistler, who commanded the division for the rest of the war apart from the period between

Major General G.T. Rennie was a capable rather than inspired commander, and remained in command of the British 3rd Infantry Division only to 13 June 1944, when he was wounded in the fighting north of Caen.

Major General D.C. Bullen-Smith commanded the British 51st (Highland) Infantry Division. This was the follow-up division for the British I Corps, and one of its brigades was landed on D-Day, though it took no part in the day's fighting.

22 January and 25 February 1945, when Major General A. Galloway commanded.

The 8th and 9th Infantry Brigades remained the core of the division's strength throughout the war, but the 7th Infantry Brigade (Guards) was removed on 15 September 1941 and replaced on 27 November of the same year by the 37th Independent Infantry Brigade which became the 7th Infantry Brigade on 8 December 1941. The 7th Infantry Brigade was removed on 4 June 1942 and, as noted above, the division then became the British 3rd Mixed Division on 22 June 1942 with the advent of the 33rd Tank Brigade.

In April 1943 the division reverted to standard infantry organization when the 185th Infantry Brigade arrived and the 33rd Tank Brigade was removed on the 10th and 28th of that month respectively. For the rest of the war the British 3rd Infantry Division was constituted by the 8th, 9th and 185th Infantry Brigades, which first fought together in the Normandy landing. The division remained in North-West Europe, and its battles after the Normandy landing were Caen (4-8 July 1944), Bourgebus Ridge (18-23 July 1944), Mont Pinçon (30 July-9 August 1944), the Nederrijn (17-27 September 1944), the Rhineland (8 February-10 March 1945) and the Rhine (23 March-1 April 1945).

At this point it is illuminating to consider the standard organization of the British infantry division at the time of Operation Overlord. The organization was based on an overall personnel strength of 18,347 all ranks, 4,330 vehicles together with 226 trailers, and weapons that included items ranging in size from pistols to self-propelled 40mm AA guns. The division's vehicles included 983 solo motorcycles, 495 miscellaneous cars, 31 armoured cars, 32 light reconnaissance cars, 595 carriers, 52 ambulances, 881 15-cwt trucks, 1,056 3-ton trucks and 205 miscellaneous tractors. The weapons included 1,011 pistols, 11,254 Lee Enfield rifles,

3rd Infantry Division – Divisional Troops

6,525 Sten sub-machine guns, 1,262 Bren light machine guns, 40 Vickers Mk I medium/heavy machine guns, 359 mortars (283 2-in, 60 3-in and 16 4.2-in weapons), 436 PIAT anti-tank weapons, 125 anti-aircraft guns (71 20mm towed, 36 40mm towed and 18 40mm self-propelled equipments), and 182 guns (72 25-pounder towed gun/howitzers, 32 17-pounder towed anti-tank guns and 78 towed 6-pounder towed anti-tank guns).

Divisional command was exercised from the Divisional HQ, where the divisional commander and his staff enjoyed the support of specialists of several types as well as the Divisional HQ Defence and Employment Platoon and the Divisional Field Security Section. Subordinate to the Divisional HQ were the formation's three organic infantry brigades, the organic divisional troops and any attached units. Each infantry brigade was based on a Brigade HQ with its own Infantry Brigade HQ Ground Defence Platoon, three infantry battalions and one non-armoured Light Aid Detachment 'Type A'. The infantry battalion had an establishment strength of 35 officers and 786 other ranks in one support company and four rifle companies. The support company comprised a mortar platoon with six 3-in mortars, a carrier platoon with 13 Universal (or Bren) Carriers, an anti-tank platoon with six towed 6-pounder guns, and an assault pioneer platoon. The rifle company had three platoons each of three sections: the section comprised 10 men and one Bren light machine gun, the platoon had one officer and 36 other ranks together with one 2-in mortar, and the company possessed five officers and 122 other ranks together with three PIAT anti-tank weapons at company HQ.

The overall capabilities of the infantry brigades were greatly bolstered by the availability of the organic divisional troops controlled by Divisional HQ for divisional purposes including support of the subordinate brigades as and when required. In descending order of precedence, the elements of the organic divisional troops were provided by the Royal Armoured Corps, Royal Artillery, Corps of Royal Engineers, Royal Corps of Signals, Infantry, Royal Army Service Corps, Royal Army Medical Corps, Royal Army Ordnance Corps, Corps of Royal Electrical and Mechanical Engineers, and Corps of Military Police. The task of the Royal Armoured Corps in this context was the rapid provision of the accurate reconnaissance data that was of vital importance to the control of operations at divisional level, and the divisional organic troops included an armoured reconnaissance regiment with its own armoured Light Aid Detachment 'Type A': however, the British 3rd Infantry Division's 3rd Reconnaissance Regiment was not formed and reconnaissance was therefore provided by non-organic sources.

The Royal Artillery provided artillery fire support as well as protection against armoured

---

ORGANIC DIVISIONAL TROOPS

HQ 3rd Infantry Division

Royal Artillery
7th Field Regiment (Self-Propelled), 9th, 16th and 17/43rd Batteries
33rd Field Regiment (Self-Propelled), 101st, 109th and 113/114th Batteries
76th Field Regiment (Self-Propelled), 302nd, 330th and 454th Batteries
20th Anti-tank Regiment, 41st, 45th, 67th and 101st Batteries

Royal Engineers
17th, 246th and 253rd Field Companies

Royal Signals
3rd Divisional Signals

Infantry
2nd Battalion, The Middlesex Regiment (Machine Gun)

Royal Army Medical Corps
8th, 9th and 223rd Field Ambulances

Military Police Corps
3rd Divisional Provost Company

The Middlesex Regiment

and air attack: its primary contribution was thus provided through the HQ Division Royal Artillery by three field regiments of towed 25-pounder gun/howitzers (each regiment comprising three batteries of two troops of four 25-pounder gun/howitzers for a regimental strength of 24 gun/howitzers with 144 HE, 16 smoke and 12 armour-piercing rounds of ammunition per equipment) and supported by their own three non-armoured Light Aid Detachments 'Type A', one anti-tank regiment with towed anti-tank guns (four batteries each comprising one troop of 6-pounder guns and two troops of 17-pounder guns for a regimental strength of 48 guns) and supported by its own non-armoured Light Aid Detachment 'Type A', and one light anti-aircraft regiment (three batteries each of three troops of six self-propelled 40mm AA guns for a regimental strength of 54 guns) and supported by its own Workshop 'Type A'.

The Royal Engineers provided all types of engineering support: its primary contribution was thus provided through the HQ Division Royal Engineers by one field parks and one divisional bridging platoon supported by their own non-armoured Light Aid Detachment 'Type A'. The Royal Signals provided communication facilities to higher as well as lower echelons via the Divisional Signals supported by its own non-armoured Light Aid Detachment 'Type B'. The divisional infantry unit was designed to provide the infantry brigades with battlefield fire support heavier than could be generated by their own weapons, and comprised one specialized machine gun battalion (35 officers and 782 other ranks with one heavy mortar company of four platoons each with four 4.2-in mortars, and three machine gun companies each of three platoons with a total of 12 Vickers Mk I medium/heavy machine guns) supported by a non-armoured Light Aid Detachment 'Type B'.

The Royal Army Service Corps provided transport capacity via the HQ Division RASC, and its main elements were the divisional troops company and three infantry brigade companies. The Royal Army Medical Corps was tasked with the treatment of battle and other casualties, and contributed three field ambulances, two forward dressing stations and one food hygiene section. The Royal Army Ordnance Corps was responsible for all ordnance matters, and provided one infantry division ordnance field park. A host of vital maintenance capabilities was generated by the Royal Electrical and Mechanical Engineers provided, via the HQ Division REME, three infantry brigade workshops. The Military Police provided one divisional provost company for the traffic control and the maintenance of order. Finally there was the divisonal postal unit, ranking low in the divisional pecking order perhaps but of singular importance in the maintenance of the men's morale.

The establishment of organic divisional troops was not always implemented in full or, as was the case in the British 3rd Infantry Division and other formations involved in the Normandy landings, supplemented for improved capabilities under specific operational conditions by additional elements from several branches of the army. In this respect the British 3rd Infantry Division was typical, for though its organic divisional troops were reduced from establishment, they were supplemented by units and also by sub-area units, both of them under command for the assault phase. The former included two units of Major General Sir Percy Hobart's British 79th Armoured Division, the formation controlled at army group level and used to provide specialized armour: the 22nd Dragoons of the 30th Armoured Brigade were equipped with flail tanks for the clearance of paths through minefields, and the 5th Engineer Assault Regiment of the 1st Assault Brigade, Royal Engineers, was equipped with several types of specialized vehicles.

The British 3rd Infantry Division was also upgraded in overall battlefield capabilities by the attachment of the 27th Armoured Brigade. This had a personnel strength of about 3,400 all ranks in three battalions. The fighting vehicle strength was about 190 Sherman medium tanks and 33 Stuart (otherwise 'Honey') light tanks. The armoured brigades attached to the infantry divisions for Operation Overlord were trained primarily for close co-operation with their associated infantry divisions during the assault phase, though they were also capable of operating with the armoured divisions once these had been delivered to play their part in the development and exploitation of the Normandy lodgement.

The sub-area units which were under command of the British 3rd Infantry Division for the assault

UNITS UNDER COMMAND FOR THE ASSAULT PHASE

Royal Armoured Corps
22nd Dragoons

Royal Artillery
HQ 53rd Medium Regiment
HQ and 218th Battery, 73rd Light Anti-Aircraft Regiment
one troop of the 318th Battery, 92nd Light Anti-Aircraft Regiment
332nd Battery, 93rd Light Anti-Aircraft Regiment
Survey Battery, 9th Survey Regiment
'B' Flight, 652nd Air Observation Post Regiment

Royal Engineers
HQ 5th Engineer Assault Regiment
77th and 79th Assault Squadrons
71st and 263rd Field Companies
629th Field Squadron

Royal Marines
No. 41 Royal Marine Commando [of the 4th Special Service Brigade]
three troops of the 5th Independent Armoured Support Battery (Self-Propelled)

Royal Army Service Corps
106th Brigade Company
90th Armoured Brigade Company

SUB-AREA UNITS UNDER COMMAND FOR THE ASSAULT PHASE

101st Beach Sub-Area
HQ and Signals Section
5th and 6th Beach Groups

Royal Engineers
HQ 18th GHQ Troops Engineers
84th and 91st Field Companies
8th and 9th Stores Sections
50th Mechanised Equipment Section
9th Port Operating Group
999th and 1028th Port Operating Companies
940th Inland Water Transport Operating Company

Infantry
5th Battalion, The King's Regiment (Liverpool)
1st Battalion, The Oxfordshire and Buckinghamshire Light Infantry

Royal Army Service Corps
HQ 21st Transport Column
39th, 101st, 299th and 633rd General Transport Companies
96th and 138th Detail Issue Depots
237th and 238th Petrol Depots

Royal Army Medical Corps
16th Casualty Clearing Station
9th, 12th, 20th, 21st and 30th Field Dressing Stations
Nos 37, 38, 39, 40 and 55 Field Surgical Units
Nos 21, 22 and 29 Field Transfusion Units
1st and 2nd Field Sanitary Sections
20th Port Detachment

Royal Army Ordnance Corps
11th and 12th Ordnance Beach Detachments
44th Ordnance Ammunition Company

Royal Electrical and Mechanical Engineers
20th and 21st Beach Recovery Sections

Military Police Corps
241st and 245th Provost Companies

Pioneer Corps
53rd, 85th, 102nd, 129th, 149th, 267th, 292nd and 303rd
Pioneer Companies

GHQ Liaison Regiment
[Five 'Phantom' patrols were ashore by the evening of 6 June in the
British Second Army sector.]

some 4,000 to 5,000 men strong complete with its Royal Navy and Royal Air Force attachments. The 'beach groups' on each assault beach were soon joined into a 'beach sub-area' for each divisional area. Each of these beach groups contained RE, RASC, RAMC and other specialist units as well as one or more infantry battalions.

A battalion commander was the beach group commander, and his first task was the elimination of any German positions bypassed by the assault forces as they pushed inland, for such positions could and did inflict serious losses on the men ensuring the arrival of the equipment and stores required as the front line was pushed inland. Once resistance had been overwhelmed, the beach group commander used his men to provide working parties for the support of the specialist units unloading stores and vehicles, clearing beach defences and wreckage, recovering drowned or damaged vehicles, establishing dumps and depots, developing beach exits and lateral roads, establishing medical facilities, and controlling traffic flow on and off the beach. On Sword Beach, overall control was exercised by the 101st Beach Sub-Area with the 5th Beach Group (based on a battalion of the King's Regiment [Liverpool]) as its primary beach group and the 6th Beach Group (based on a battalion of the Oxfordshire and Buckinghamshire Light Infantry) as its reserve.

phase of Operation Overlord were concerned with the organization of matters on the beach. Control of incoming and outgoing ships and craft was the responsibility of Royal Navy parties commanded by a beachmaster, but the movement of men, equipment and supplies across and off the congested beaches was controlled by the army. At first the army organization was the 'beach group', a loosely organized unit soon

51st (Highland) Infantry Division

The British 51st (Highland) Infantry Division was an organic part of the British I Corps, and earmarked to follow the British 3rd Infantry Division across Sword Beach. The division was gathered in Essex and embarked at Southend, but only its 153rd Infantry Brigade arrived under command of Brigadier H. Murray on D-Day's second tide, and in the event took no part in the day's fighting.

Commanded by Major General D.C. Bullen-Smith, the British 51st (Highland) Infantry Division was another formation with some pedigree, for it was already in existence at the beginning of World War II as a first-line Territorial Army division with the 152nd, 153rd and 154th Infantry Brigades. The division moved to France from 24 January 1940 under the command of Major General V.M. Fortune, became heavily involved in the Battle of France and, less its 154th Infantry Brigade, was captured on 12 June 1940.

A new 51st (Highland) Division was created on 7 August 1940 by the redesignation of Major General A.G. Cunningham's 9th (Highland) Infantry Division together with its 26th, 27th and 28th Infantry Brigades: the first two became the 152nd and 153rd Infantry Brigades, and the last was absorbed into the 154th Infantry Brigade that had escaped from the French débâcle. In June 1942 the division was shipped to North Africa under command of Major General D.N.

153rd Infantry Brigade
[landed on the evening of 6 June under command of the 3rd Infantry Division]

5th Battalion, The Black Watch
1st Battalion, The Gordon Highlanders
5/7th Battalion, The Gordon Highlanders

The Gordon Highlanders

The Black Watch

Wimberley. In this theatre the division was part of the British Eighth Army's XIII, XXX and X Corps, and played a distinguished part in the Battles of El Alamein (23 October-4 November 1942), Medenine (6 March 1943), the Mareth Line (16-23 March 1943), Akarit (6-7 April 1943), Enfidaville (19-29 April 1943) and Tunis (5-12 May 1943). The division was then used in the Sicilian operation as part of XXX Corps, being involved in the Landing in Sicily (9-12 July 1943) and the Adrano (29 July-3 August) battles. Now commanded by Bullen-Court, the division was shipped back to the UK in November 1943.

The division's two battles in Normandy were Bourgebus Ridge (18-23 July 1944) and Falaise (7-22 August 1944). The division then came under various British, Canadian and even American corps commands before re-entering combat, where its battles were the Rhineland (8 February-10 March 1945) and the Rhine (23 March-1 April 1945). On 26 July 1944 command of the division had passed to Major General T.G. Rennie, but this officer was killed on 24 March 1945 and on the following day Major General G.H.A. MacMillan assumed command for the rest of the war.

8th Infantry Brigade

The 8th Infantry Brigade was already in existence at the start of World War II as a unit of the regular army in the UK, and remained a component of the 3rd Infantry Division throughout the war. The 8th Infantry Brigade's three infantry battalions at the beginning of hostilities were the 1st Battalion, The Suffolk Regiment, the 2nd Battalion, The East Yorkshire Regiment (The Duke of York's Own) and the 2nd Battalion, The Gloucester Regiment together with the 8th Infantry Brigade Attack Company.

Under the command of Brigadier F.H. Witts, the brigade moved to France on 1 November 1939. On 2 February 1940 the Glosters were replaced by the 4th Battalion, The Royal Berkshire Regiment (Princess Charlotte of Wales's). Command of the brigade was assumed on 21 February by Brigadier C.G. Woolner, succeeded on 3 November by Lieutenant Colonel T.F. Given (acting) who gave way on 27 November to Brigadier G. Symes. Symes commanded during the French campaign, when the brigade saw action in the Ypres and Comines Canal sector between 26 and 28 May before falling back to Dunkirk, from where it was evacuated on 31 May.

The brigade re-formed in the UK, and later changes were the replacement of the Royal Berks by the 1st Battalion, The South Lancashire Regiment (The Prince of Wales's Volunteers) on 11 June 1940 and the removal of the 8th Infantry

The Suffolk Regiment

The East Yorkshire Regiment

The South Lancashire Regiment

Brigade Attack Company on 1 January 1941. Command of the brigade passed to Brigadier Hon. W. Fraser on 26 June 1941, Brigadier B.W.S. Cripps on 3 March 1942, and then Brigadier E.E.E. Cass on 7 October 1943.

It was in this form that the brigade was earmarked as the leading element of the British Second Army's 3rd Infantry Division for the landing on Sword Beach during Operation Overlord on 6 June 1944. Thereafter the brigade remained in North-West Europe, and its battles in this period were those of the division at Caen (4-8 July 1944), Bourgebus Ridge (18-23 July 1944), Mont Pincon (30 July-9 August 1944), the Nederrijn (17-27 September 1944), the Rhineland (8 February-10 March 1945) and the Rhine (23 March-1 April 1945). Command was exercised during this period by Cass, Lieutenant Colonel M.A. Foster (acting, 13-23 June 1944), Cass again, and then Brigadier E.H. Goulburn (from 27 October 1944). The brigade remained in Germany after the end of hostilities for occupation duties.

8th INFANTRY BRIGADE
(Brigadier E.E.E. Cass)

1st Battalion, The Suffolk Regiment
2nd Battalion, The East Yorkshire Regiment (Duke of York's Own)
1st Battalion, The South Lancashire Regiment (Prince of Wales's Volunteers)

9th Infantry Brigade

The 9th Infantry Brigade was already in existence at the start of World War II as a unit of the regular army in the UK, and remained a component of the 3rd Infantry Division (from June 1942 to April 1943 the 3rd Mixed Division with one tank brigade) throughout the war. The 9th Infantry Brigade's three infantry battalions at the start of hostilities were the 2nd Battalion, The Royal Lincolnshire Regiment, the 1st Battalion, The King's Own Scottish Borderers and the 2nd Battalion, The Royal Ulster Rifles together with the 9th Infantry Brigade Attack Company.

Under command of Brigadier W. Robb the brigade moved to France on 4 October 1939. Robb led the brigade during the French campaign of May 1940, when the brigade saw action in the Ypres and Comines Canal sector between 26 and 28 May, and then fell back to Dunkirk, from which its survivors were evacuated to the UK on 31 May. The brigade re-formed in the UK, and the only later change was the removal of the 9th Infantry Brigade Attack Company on 1 January 1941. Command of the brigade passed to Brigadier B.G. Horrocks on 17 June 1940, to Brigadier J.F. Hare on 4 February 1941, to Brigadier T.N.F. Wilson on 19 March 1942, as a temporary measure to Lieutenant Colonel P. Reid on 4 July 1942, and then to Brigadier J.C. Cunningham on 18 July 1942.

The Lincolnshire Regiment

The King's Own Scottish Borders

The Royal Ulster Rifles

It was under Cunningham's command that the brigade was allocated the task of coming ashore as the third and final element of the British Second Army's 3rd Infantry Division for the landing on Sword Beach during Operation Overlord on 6 June 1944. Thereafter the brigade remained in North-West Europe as partner to the 8th and 185th Infantry Brigades in the 3rd Infantry Division, and its battles in this period were those of the division at Caen (4-18 July 1944), Bourgebus Ridge (18-23 July 1944), Mont Pincon (30 July-9 August 1944), the Nederrijn (17-27 September 1944), the Rhineland (8 February-10 March 1945) and the Rhine (23 March-1 April 1945). Cunningham was badly wounded on 6 June 1944 and was succeeded from the following day by Brigadier A.D.G. Orr. Later commanders were Brigadier G.D. Browne from 9 August 1944, Brigadier G.D. Renny from 1 January 1945 and Brigadier W.F.H. Kempster from 1 April 1945. The brigade remained in Germany after the end of hostilities for occupation duties, and returned to the UK on 31 August 1945.

9th INFANTRY BRIGADE
(Brigadier J.C. Cunningham)

2nd Battalion, The Lincolnshire Regiment
1st Battalion, The King's Own Scottish Borderers
2nd Battalion, The Royal Ulster Rifles

185th Infantry Brigade

The 185th Infantry Brigade came into existence on 1 September 1942 by the redesignation of the 204th Independent Infantry Brigade (Home), which had been created in October 1940 for service in the UK by No.4 Infantry Training Group. The new brigade was initially allocated to the Durham & North Riding Area HQ, and received its first infantry battalion only eight days after its creation, which was the date on which the brigade was allocated to the British 79th Armoured Division. This first unit was the 2nd Battalion, The King's Shropshire Light Infantry, and this initial battalion was joined on the following day by the 2nd Battalion, The Royal Warwickshire Fusiliers and the 1st Battalion, The Royal Norfolk Regiment to complete the brigade's strength of three infantry battalions. The same three battalions remained with the brigade for the rest of World War II.

On 10 April 1943 the British 79th Armoured Division was switched to the development of specialized armour and the techniques for its use, and as such lost its organic infantry brigade. The 185th Infantry Brigade thus became the third infantry brigade of the British 3rd Infantry Division on the latter's reversion to infantry from mixed organizational status. The brigade was commanded from 4 June 1943 by Lieutenant Colonel N.C.S. Smith (acting) and from the 17th of the same month by Brigadier K.P. Smith, who

The Royal Warwickshire Fusiliers

The Royal Norfolk Regiment

The King's Shropshire Light Infantry

led the brigade during the early stages of the Normandy fighting, when the brigade was landed as the second of its division's three brigades on Sword Beach on 6 June 1944.

Thereafter the brigade remained in North-West Europe in the 3rd Infantry Division, and its battles in this period were those of the division at Caen (4-18 July 1944), Bourgebus Ridge (18-23 July 1944), Mont Pincon (30 July-9 August 1944), the Nederrijn (17-27 September 1944), the Rhineland (8 February-10 March 1945) and the Rhine (23 March-1 April 1945). Smith was replaced in command on 2 July 1944 by Brigadier E.L. Bols, and later commanders were Brigadier E.H.G. Grant from 11 December 1944, Lieutenant Colonel D.L.A. Gibbs (acting) from 15 January 1945, Lieutenant Colonel F.P. Barclay (acting) from 19 January 1945, and Brigadier F.R.G. Matthews from 20 January 1945 for the rest of the war.

The brigade remained in Germany after the end of hostilities for occupation duties under the command of Brigadier R.N.H.C. Bray from 7 June 1945.

185th INFANTRY BRIGADE
(Brigadier K.P. Smith)

2nd Battalion, The Royal Warwickshire Fusiliers
1st Battalion, The Royal Norfolk Regiment
2nd Battalion, The King's Shropshire Light Infantry

27th Armoured Brigade

The 27th Armoured Brigade came into existence on 26 November 1940 by the redesignation of the 1st Armoured Reconnaissance Brigade, which had been created in France on 30 March 1940 under the command of Brigadier C.W. Norman. The new brigade was initially controlled by the GHQ of the British Expeditionary Force, but later by the British I Corps, Macforce and the British 48th Infantry Division. The brigade's initial strength was only the 1st East Riding Yeomanry, but this was joined on 7 April 1940 by the 1st Fife and Forfar Yeomanry. The brigade was evacuated from Dunkirk on 30 May 1940 and re-formed in the UK with the Fife and Forfar Yeomanry replaced from 18 June 1940 by the 4th/7th Royal Dragoon Guards and the 13th/18th Hussars, which raised the brigade to a strength of three regiments. The brigade was controlled in the UK by Southern Command and then Eastern Command, and after becoming the 27th Armoured Brigade by the British IV Corps, the British 9th Armoured Division and Eastern Command before passing to the British 79th Armoured Division between 8 September 1942 and 8 October 1943.

Brigade commanders during this period were Norman, Brigadier H.F. Fisher from 15 October 1941, Brigadier J.G. de W. Mullens from 1 March 1942 and Brigadier G.E. Prior-Palmer from 25 April 1943. From 2 December 1940 the brigade

13th/18th Royal Hussars

The Staffordshire Yeomanry

also contained a motorized infantry battalion in the form of the 1st Battalion, Queen Victoria's Rifles though this was replaced on 1 April 1941 by the 7th Battalion, The King's Royal Rifle Corps: the motorized infantry battalion was removed from the brigade's establishment on 13 April 1943. Between 8 October 1943 and 31 January 1944 the East Riding Yeomanry was replaced by the 148th Regiment RAC, and the brigade reached its definitive D-Day form on 14 February 1944 when the Staffordshire Yeomanry arrived to replace the 4th/7th Royal Dragoon Guards.

The 27th Armoured Brigade was attached to the British 3rd Infantry Division on 20 October 1943, and fought with this division during the Normandy landings. On 3 July 1944 the brigade was taken under command of the British I Corps, and fought under its command in the Caen battle (4-18 July 1944).

27th ARMOURED BRIGADE
(Brigadier G.E. Prior-Palmer)

13th/18th Royal Hussars (Queen Mary's Own)
The East Riding Yeomanry
The Staffordshire Yeomanry

1st and 4th Special Service Brigades

In the months after the Allied evacuation from Dunkirk in the first days of June 1940, and the fall of France to German invasion by the end of the same month, there was every reason to suppose that Germany's next military move would be an invasion of the UK. Disorganized and short of heavy weapons after the débâcle in France, the British army scrambled to re-create a field army that could stem and then repulse any German invasion. In these dire months thought was given to many defensive expedients, some of them practical but most of them impractical.

Prime Minister Winston Churchill tended toward a belief in such expedients, and he and his advisers decided in June 1940 that 'There ought to be at least twenty thousand Storm Troops or "Leopards" drawn from existing units, ready to spring at the throats of any small landings or descents'. Churchill's thinking in this matter was based on the use of small groups of highly trained but lightly equipped troops to strike at the enemy's rear areas and communications, and Churchill eagerly endorsed a more precise appreciation of the capabilities of such parties prepared by Lieutenant Colonel Dudley Clarke, the military assistant to General Sir John Dill, the Chief of the Imperial General Staff. Churchill directed that an immediate start should be made on the creation of such forces, which received the name Commandos and were each to be based on a structure of 10 troops each comprising three officers and 47 men equipped with weapons that were not essential for the defence of the UK against German invasion. Selection emphasis was placed on youth, and among the qualities demanded from volunteers were 'courage, physical endurance, initiative and resource, activity, marksmanship, self-reliance, and an aggressive spirit towards the war' together with a willingness to become 'accustomed to longer hours, more work, and less rest than the regular members of His Majesty's Forces, and [such men] must also become expert in all the military uses of scouting – ability to stalk, to notice and report on everything taking place in their vicinity, to move across any type of country by day or by night, silently and unseen, and to live "off the country" for a considerable period'.

A good starting point for the new force was the independent companies raised from Territorial Army units for service in Norway, and Nos 1 and 2 Commandos were raised from this source. There followed another 10 Commandos. Most of these were created in June 1940, but the last was raised in January 1942 as No.10 Commando with Belgian, Dutch, French and Norwegian personnel. By October 1940 the German invasion threat was receding, and with it the need for the Commandos to be trained primarily for defensive warfare. This accorded well with Churchill's insistent demand that the war be taken to the Germans, even if this was only on a small scale. The Commandos were thus reoriented toward

Lovats Scouts

offensive warfare, most notably in the form of seaborne raids on coastal targets in German-occupied Europe. The first such raid was mounted on 23-24 June 1940, when a force of 120 men was landed on the French coast near Boulogne, faced some German troops in a small firefight, and then withdrew. A raid on occupied Guernsey followed on 14-15 July 1940, when 100 men of No.11 Independent Company and 40 men of No.3 Commando were to attack the island's airfield: the Commandos landed in the right place, found no opposition and withdrew, but the men of the Independent Company suffered an embarrassing failure when two of their four launches broke down on the outward leg from Portsmouth, the third ran aground, and the fourth suffered a navigational error and landed on Sark! Churchill was furious, and minuted 'Let there be no more silly fiascos like that perpetrated at Guernsey. The idea of working all these coasts up against us by pinprick raids is one to be strictly avoided'.

This revised concept of offensive operations suggested that the standard 500-man Commando of 10 50-man troops was too unwieldy, so an October 1940 reorganization created, within Admiral of the Fleet Sir Roger Keyes' Combined Operations Headquarters organization, the Special Service Brigade commanded by Brigadier J.C. Haydon and consisting of four Special Service battalions, each comprising a battalion HQ and two Commandos. Further change followed in March 1941, when the Special Service battalions were reorganized as Commandos, each comprising five troops of three officers and 62 men together with a heavy weapons troop of about 40 men. The same month also saw the first genuinely successful Commando raid, when some 600 men (Nos 3 and 4 Commandos with about 250 men each, 52 Royal Engineers trained in demolition work, and 52 Norwegian guides) landed on three of the German-occupied Lofoten Islands off Norway on 4 March 1941: the raid netted 216 German prisoners and 11 ships captured, brought back 314 Norwegian volunteers, and resulted in the demolition of the islands' 18 fish oil factories and the destruction of more than 800,000 gallons of fuel.

Further raids enjoyed greater or lesser success,

1st SPECIAL SERVICE BRIGADE
(Brigadier Lord Lovat)

No. 3 Commando
No. 4 Commando
No. 6 Commando
No. 45 Royal Marine Commando
  two troops of No. 10 (Inter-Allied) Commando
  one troop of the Royal Marine Engineer Commando
Brigade Signal Troop
Light Aid Detachment Type A

but Keyes was at increasing loggerheads with the Chiefs-of-Staff and, in his capacity as a Member of Parliament, with the Cabinet. It is hardly surprising, therefore, that on 10 October 1941 Admiral Keyes was replaced by Admiral Lord Louis Mountbatten as Director of Combined Operations with the task not just of continuing Commando operations but also, and considerably more importantly, of creating the amphibious warfare techniques that would allow the Allies eventually to undertake the major landing in France that would preface their final and total defeat of Germany. Keyes had already started moving in this direction with the expedition to the Norwegian island of Spitzbergen between 25 August and 3 September 1941. The island contains huge coal deposits that were worked mainly by a Soviet organization using Soviet labour. After the German invasion of the USSR on 22 June 1941, it seemed sensible to prevent these important strategic assets from German exploitation. A garrison was clearly impractical, and Keyes decided that the next best thing would be the destruction of the mines and all stockpiled coal. A raiding party of Canadian infantry was complemented by Royal Engineer and Norwegian parties, all ferried to the island under Royal Navy escort. The operation met no opposition, rescued 2,000 Soviet and 800 Norwegian civilians of whom the former were ferried to Murmansk and the latter brought back to the UK together with 200 French prisoners of war who had escaped to the USSR, destroyed the coal mines, and burned 540,000 tons of coal and 275,000 gallons of fuel. This success was followed on 27 December 1941 by another raid on the Lofoten Islands, where a force of 51 officers and 525 men drawn from four Commandos caused great damage on Vaagso as their escorting warships sank some 16,000 tons of German shipping.

Other raids followed, allowing the British and their allies to gain and develop considerable expertise in the art of landind on an occupied coast. These landings were all on a small scale, however, and it took the tactical disaster of Operation Jubilee to provide a lesson about the futility of trying to land a major formation directly into an occupied port. Undertaken on 18 August 1942, 'Jubilee' landed the Canadian 2nd Infantry Division, supported on its flanks by Nos 3 and 4 Commandos, on the beach of Dieppe on the French side of the English Channel. The assault forces could make no real headway into the town, and were evacuated after the loss of 3,363 Canadians and 247 Commandos. The Dieppe raid certainly bloodied the Anglo-Canadian nose, but its lessons were of vital importance in creating the tactics that worked so well in the Normandy landings.

Operational experience now brought about a further revision of the Commando organization in the spring of 1943. In this revision the Special Service Brigade, commanded by Brigadier R.E. Laycock, was divided into five active groups as well as the Brigade Signal Troop and the Commando Depot Mountain and Snow Warfare Camp.

The active groups each comprised a group HQ and one or more Commandos: the groups comprised firstly Nos 1, 3 and 6 Commandos, secondly Nos 2, 4, 5, 9 and 12 Commandos, thirdly Nos 40 and 41 Royal Marine Commandos, fourthly No.10 (Inter-Allied) Commando, and fifthly Nos 14, 30 and 62 Commandos together with the Special Boat Section and the Combined Operations Pilotage Parties. Further expansion of Commando capabilities meant that this organization was obsolete by November 1943, and the Commando Forces Headquarters ordered that the Special Service Brigade should become the Special Service Group under command of Major General R.G. Sturges. This was in effect a Commando divisional HQ and controlled a number of organic specialist units as well as four Special Service brigades each with a Brigade Signal Troop and a Light Aid Detachment 'Type A'. The specialist units fell into three groups, comprising firstly the Group Signals, Field Security Section, Repair Section Light Aid Detachment 'Type A', Provost Section and Postal Unit Section, secondly the all-arms Special Boat Unit and the Royal Marine Engineer Commando, and thirdly the Group 2nd Echelon (Royal Marine only), Holding Commando, Commando Basic Training Centre and Commando Mountain Warfare Training Centre.

The two Special Service brigades in the UK were the 1st and 4th Special Service Brigades commanded respectively by Brigadier Lord Lovat and Brigadier B.W. Leicester: the 1st Special Service Brigade comprised Nos 3, 4, 6 and 45 (Royal Marine) Commandos, while the 4th Special Service Brigade comprised Nos 41 (Royal Marine), 46 (Royal Marine), 47 (Royal Marine) and 10 (Inter-Allied) Commandos; in March 1944 No.48 (Royal Marine) Commando was created, and this replaced No.10 (Inter-Allied) Commando in the 4th Special Service Brigade during April 1944. In Italy was Brigadier T.D.L.C. Churchill's 2nd Special Service Brigade with Nos 2, 9, 40 (Royal Marine) and 43 (Royal Marine) Commandos. And finally in India was Brigadier D.I. Nonweiler's 3rd Special Service Brigade with Nos 1, 5, 42 (Royal Marine) and 44 (Royal Marine) Commandos.

4th SPECIAL SERVICE BRIGADE
(Brigadier B.W. Leicester)

No. 41 Royal Marine Commando [under command of the 3rd Infantry Division]
No. 46 Royal Marine Commando [landed after D-Day]
No. 47 Royal Marine Commando [landed after D-Day]
No. 48 Royal Marine Commando [under command of the Canadian 3rd Infantry Division]
one troop of the Royal Marine Engineer Commando [under command of the Canadian 3rd Infantry Division]
three troops of the 5th Independent Armoured Support Battery [under command of the 3rd Infantry Division]
Brigade Signal Troop
Light Aid Detachment Type A

8th Infantry & 27th Armoured Brigades

In the early morning of 6 June, the convoys carrying the assault forces for Operation Overlord approached the Normandy coast. Many of the men, naval as well as military, had been affected by sea-sickness as a result of the rough seas now subsiding from their gale-swept worst, but most of the assault troops could hear or see the activities of the bombers and naval units giving the German defences a last pounding. The British 3rd Infantry Division heading for Sword Beach was carried by Convoy S under the supervision of Rear Admiral A.G. Talbot in the command ship *Largs*, and from her bridge Talbot and his staff could see that the convoy had reached the right position at the correct time, the only problems being the straggling of a few ships that were now making up for lost time, and the loss of some landing craft as they made their way from the English south coast in tow or under their own power. Most of the few craft lost had been those carrying heavy equipment such as the tanks of the Royal Marine Armoured Support Regiment and the heavy mortars and 60-lb spigot mortars required to blast lanes through the beach mine-fields.

About eight miles from Sword Beach the convoy halted and the troops started to clamber down the nets from the ships into their landing craft. Already the first wave of craft was moving off to launch its vanguard force of Sherman Duplex Drive amphibious tanks at a point closer to the shore. Behind the tanks, successive waves of landing craft carried the assault infantry, assault engineers with their armoured vehicles, self-propelled artillery, and then additional forces of armour, infantry, engineers, artillery together with the first elements of the mass of support equipment that would be landed as soon as the assault forces had secured the beach.

The last bombers were already departing after giving the beach defences their final attention, and as the landing craft approached the beach the guns of the naval bombardment forces switched from beach to inland and flank targets, leaving the defences to be given a final pasting by the massed rockets carried by specially modified landing craft, and by the field artillery and tanks carried by another series of landing craft designed to allow their embarked weapons to engage the enemy while still afloat. As the landing craft closed the shore and the fire of the assault forces and their naval support units was re-registered to more distant targets, it became clear that not all the German beach positions had been crushed. The defenders scrambled from their bunkers as the British fire switched to targets farther afield, manned their guns and mortars, and began to engage the landing craft as they approached the beach. These craft were comparatively difficult targets while they were on

the move, but once beached they were easier targets. Large numbers of landing craft were now hit, and the mass of British troops, vehicles and equipment ploughing through the surf and the shallower water on the edge of the beach began to suffer from the fire of the German guns and mortars, which were now supplemented in their efforts by machine guns.

The landing had been timed for low water so that the incoming tide would refloat the landing craft, and the heavily-laden assault forces were faced by a dangerous and sometimes long progress over a fire-swept beach. The plan called for amphibious tanks, flail tanks, Armoured Vehicles Royal Engineer, obstacle-clearance groups, infantry and assault engineers to arrive within minutes of each other, but precise adherence to such co-ordination was impossble. In some spots the Sherman DD tanks arrived first, but in others it was obstacle clearance groups, assault engineers with their AVREs, flail tanks or infantry. Soon naval parties were tackling the mine-protected beach obstacles covered by the incoming tide while Royal Engineers dealt with those still above water, the flail tanks were beating paths through possible minefields for the infantry, and the AVREs were battering or bridging their way forward to create exits off the beaches for the infantry and mass of vehicles.

The forces undertaking these tasks were often under enfilading fire, and the number of men and vehicles hit gradually swelled. In several areas the infantry did not wait for these preliminary tasks to be completed, but rushed across the beaches to find cover under the dunes or beach walls and then fanned out in search of the German positions pouring down the enfilading fire. The infantry soon received the support of the tanks that managed to cross the beach, and further capability against the German defences was provided by low-flying fighters and rocket-armed Hawker Typhoon fighter-bombers.

The 8th Infantry Brigade was the assault element of the British 3rd Infantry Division's Sword Beach landing, and its experience during the assault phase was essentially similar to that of the other assault forces, though the fire of the escorting destroyers and other support craft was so effective that little German resistance was encountered until the landing craft were quite close inshore. The infantry assault units were the 2nd East Yorkshire on the left and 1st South Lancashire on the right of the Queen assault area between la Brèche and Lion-sur-Mer, but these two battalions were to be preceded by the specialized armour of another unit, the 13th/18th Hussars, and then enjoy the armoured support of elements from two other regiments, namely one squadron of the 22nd Dragoons and two (later three) squadrons of the 5th Independent

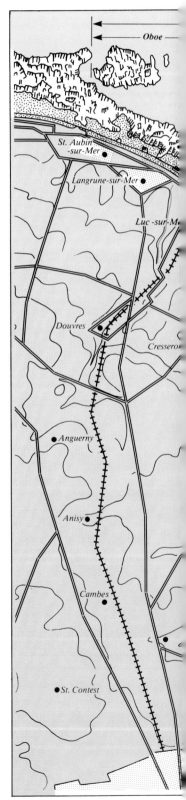

Battery, Royal Marine Armoured Support Regiment. The 13th/18th Hussars had 40 Sherman DD tanks, and 34 of these were launched at sea: two were lost at sea, six in the surf and another four shortly after this, leaving the regiment with 28 tanks after the 22 survivors of the offshore launch had been supplemented by six that came ashore from their landing craft. The 13th/18th Hussars did not reach the beach of the Queen assault area before the infantry, however, so the landing was started at 0726 hours, just one minute behind schedule, by two troops of the 5th

Independent Battery, the 22nd Dragoons, and the defence-breaching teams. Such was the strength of the onshore wind that the obstacle-clearance groups could mark only one clear lane through the beach defences before the advancing tide covered the rest until the next ebb. The conditions were so bad that the obstacle clearing parties were soon exhausted, and several sappers were swept away. In the circumstances, the landing craft had to come ashore as best they could, and there were inevitably many losses.

The leading elements of the two infantry assault battalions arrived at 0730 hours and disgorged their loads without loss, the rest of these two battalions arriving about 20 minutes later. The infantry was now faced with the task of crossing the foreshore, which had been narrowed to about 15 yards by the rising tide and was swept by fire from the German strongpoint at la Brèche. The infantry managed to reach the line of houses flanking the coastal road without too many casualties, and single companies from each battalion joined forces to clear the strongpoint at la Brèche, a task achieved in some three hours of fighting. The other companies started to clear the houses. One company of the 1st South Lancashire moved west to guard the landing's right flank, soon linking with No.41 (Royal Marine) Commando in a vain effort to take the strongpoint at Lion-sur-Mer. The bulk of the 2nd East Yorkshire moved east to protect the landing's left flank and take positions round Ouistreham, with No.4 Commando and two French troops of No.10 Commando following. The rest of the 1st South Lancs was now able to advance inland and take Hermanville sur Mer by 0900 hours.

The 8th Infantry Brigade's schedule had already been thrown out of joint by the incoming tide and continued German artillery fire. The wind-aided tide had so narrowed the foreshore that lateral movement to the beach exits was virtually impossible until the ebb had widened it, and German gunners from beyond the River Orne were able to use the beach-head barrage balloons as aiming marks until these were sensibly cut away after the threat of German air attack had failed to materialize. But before this, the 1st Suffolk had had a difficult time of it while landing as the 8th Infantry Brigade's third battalion. By the middle of the morning, therefore, the 8th Infantry Brigade had made good progress: the 1st South Lancs had taken Hermanville, the 2nd East Yorks was clearing the German positions south of Ouistreham, and the 1st Suffolk had moved forward to take Colleville-sur-Orne and was now attacking two strongpoints to the south of Coleville, known to the Allies as 'Morris' and 'Hillman'. The former contained four field guns and its 67-man garrison surrenderd as soon as the 1st Suffolk appeared, but the latter held the HQ of the German 736th Infantry Regiment and fell only after strenuous fighting at about 2000 hours that evening. There was little further movement in store for the 8th Infantry Brigade, which ended D-Day in an arc extending south-west from Hermanville in front of the road to Caen.

THE BATTLES
185th Infantry & 27th Armoured Brigades

The second element of the British 3rd Infantry Division to land was the 185th Infantry Brigade, and this started to come ashore in the middle of the morning. The brigade was a short time behind schedule, but this fact was not vitally important as its predecessor onto French soil, the 8th Infantry Brigade, was already somewhat behind schedule and was now being slowed by the German defence on the northern slope of the ridge between Périers sur le Dan and Hermanville-sur-Mer. As the brigade lost momentum, the pressure behind it increased. Elements of the British 79th Armoured Division had opened eight out of the nine planned exit lanes from Sword Beach and masses of men and equipment were coming in from the sea. But there was limited opportunity on the beach for these forces to reach their right exits, and then little space for them to occupy once they had cleared the beach, so there was inevitable but unfortunate congestion.

The 185th Infantry Brigade's three battalions had a high priority, and by 1100 hours had left the beach area to reach the brigade's allotted concentration area about half a mile inland in the orchard area near Hermanville. It was such a situation that revealed the lack of tactical experience among British commanders: if the 185th Infantry Brigade had reinforced the 8th Infantry Brigade, some of the lost momentum might have been regained and the Germans' 'Hillman' position might have been taken during the afternoon rather than the evening of 6 June, with a consequent benefit to the speed of the British advance on Caen. But the 185th Infantry Brigade had been allocated the task of leading the drive on Caen after passing through the 8th Infantry Brigade. The brigade commander decided to await his heavy weapons and armoured support before committing his brigade, and thus was lost a vital chance for a rapid breakthrough over the Périers ridge, and with it the opportunity not only for a speedy advance on Caen but also for the much-needed relief of the British 6th Airborne Division's air-head on the eastern side of the River Orne. Further delay was now occasioned by the congestion on Sword Beach, for the 185th Infantry Brigade's advance towards Caen was to be led by the 2nd KSLI riding on the tanks of the Staffordshire Yeomanry and supported by the guns of the 7th Field Regiment. The 2nd KSLI's allotment of tanks managed to get clear of the beach-head but was then delayed by a minefield, and at 1200 hours the artillery and most of the tanks and the 185th Infantry Brigade's heavy weapons were still trapped in the congestion and fretting to move inland for their tasks.

Smith finally decided that further delay was unacceptable, and at about 1230 hours the 2nd

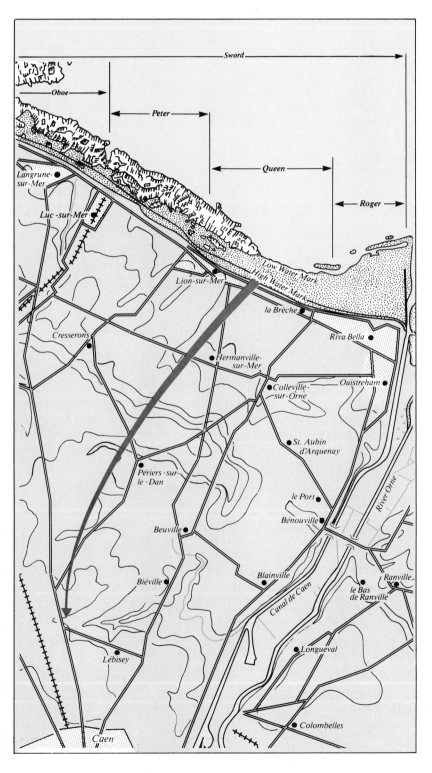

KSLI started to move south. By 1400 hours the 2nd KSLI had reached the crest of the Périers ridge. The first tanks had meanwhile caught up with the infantry and indeed overtaken the latter's leading elements, but now came under fire from the woods to their right front. Soon five of the Staffordshire Yeomanry's gun tanks and four of the Westminster Dragoons' flail tanks had been hit, and a company of infantry was diverted to support the armour as the rest of the 2nd KSLI's column continued along the road toward Caen, moving south toward Beuville and Biéville as a squadron of the Staffordshire Yeomanry occupied the tactically important height of Point 61 commanding the area around it.

The rest of the 185th Infantry Brigade, namely the 2nd Warwick and 1st Norfolk, stayed at the brigade's initial assembly point near Hermanville for several hours. At 1500 hours the 1st Norfolk was ordered to move up and secure the high ground to the left of the 2nd KSLI. The battalion commander thought that St Aubin d'Arquenay was still held by the Germans (even though the 1st Special Service Brigade had passed through it at 1200 hours), and therefore decided to move across country between St Aubin and the 'Hillman' position. The battalion lost its direction in a field of standing corn covered by the machine guns of 'Hillman', which was still untaken, and in a very short space of time suffered no fewer than 150 casualties. The battalion pressed on, however, and by 1900 hours that evening had taken the high ground between Beuville and Bénouville. The 2nd Warwick was not ordered forward until the late afternoon, and reached St Aubin at about 1800 hours.

At 1600 hours, the 185th Infantry Brigade was moving toward Caen along two axes. On the direct road from Hermanville was the 2nd KSLI at Beuville and Biéville: here the battalion was reached by its 6-pounder anti-tank guns, and further support was provided by the 17-pounder anti-tank guns of the 20th Anti-tank Regiment and the tanks of one Staffordshire Yeomanry squadron. (Of the other two Staffordshire Yeomanry squadrons, one was supporting the 1st Suffolk's attack on 'Hillman' and the other was on Périers ridge as a right-flank guard.) Farther back, and moving south-east toward the more easterly road from Ouistreham to Caen, were the brigade's other two battalions, the 1st Norfolk and 2nd Warwick.

It was at this point in the day's fighting that the first German armour was encountered. The initial indication that the British tanks were about to encounter their German opposite numbers came shortly after 1600 hours, when a forward troop of the Staffordshire Yeomanry reported seeing German tanks on the move from Caen. The Staffordshire Yeomanry squadron supporting the attack on 'Hillman' was diverted towards Biéville, and had just arrived to the west of this village when it was attacked by some 40 German tanks: the Staffordshire Yeomanry's tanks and the 2nd KSLI's anti-tank guns each knocked out

27th Armoured Brigade vehicles landing near Hermanville-sur-Mer on D-Day morning.

two of the attackers, whose surviving vehicles veered away into the apparent safety of the woods. The Staffordshire Yeomanry pursued, and further German losses resulted from tank and artillery fire. The German tanks sheered off, linked up with others and swung round toward the Périers ridge. But there they ran into the squadron of the Staffordshire Yeomanry posted in this spot for just such an eventuality. Three more German tanks were knocked out, bringing the known total to 13 but, as later revealed by German records, in fact to a higher but unspecified number. The British had lost just one self-propelled gun.

What the 185th Infantry Brigade and its tank regiment support from the 27th Armoured Brigade had met was the leading unit of Generalleutnant Edgar Feuchtinger's 21st Panzer Division, which was one of the reserve formations available to Generalfeldmarschall Erwin Rommel's Army Group 'B' and had first been committed in an attempt to contain and then to eliminate the air-head of the British 6th Airborne Division to the east of the River Orne. Arriving on French soil before the seaborne invasion had been detected, the airborne operation had attracted the Germans' initial response, and it was only later in the morning of 6 June, when the seaborne invasion had started to land and the Germans had begun to appreciate the combined armour and infantry threat to Caen, that it was decided to switch the major focus of the 21st Panzer Division's attention from the British 6th Airborne Division to the British 3rd Infantry Division.

The steadfast resistance of the 185th Infantry Brigade and its armoured support now pushed the German armour to the west, where it advanced into the gap between the British 3rd and Canadian 3rd Infantry Divisions, reaching the sea at Lion-sur-Mer before pulling back when two streams of gliders were seen heading for the area to its rear. The 21st Panzer Division halted for the night at Lebisey with only 70 effective fighting vehicles.

Once the German counter-attack near Biéville had been driven off, the 2nd KSLI resumed its movement toward Caen, but was then checked north of Lebisey by German positions in the woods on each side of the road. Dusk was approaching and there was the possibility of a renewed German tank attack on its right flank, so the battalion halted for the night around Beuville and Biéville with its leading elements some three miles short of Caen.

Meanwhile the 2nd Warwick, with the 1st Norfolk following, was continuing to push forward in the direction of Bénouville, but was slowed by the presence of German defenders in le Port, just to the north of Bénouville. The 2nd Warwick attacked at about 2100 hours, cleared le Port and then moved on Bénouville, where a party of the 7th Parachute was holding out against German counter-attacks. The 2nd Warwick relieved the airborne troops and then pushed south along the Canal de Caen before halting for the night at Blainville.

9th Infantry & 27th Armoured Brigades

The 9th Infantry Brigade was the last of the British 3rd Infantry Division's organic units to come ashore on Sword Beach during 6 June. The brigade landed somewhat behind schedule during the early afternoon of D-Day as the preceding units of the British 3rd Infantry Division sought to achieve their first objectives: the 8th Infantry Brigade was consolidating the flanks of the divisional beach-head, and the 185th Infantry Brigade was pushing inland toward Caen.

It had been planned that the 9th Infantry Brigade would assemble just inland from the beach before advancing south-west toward a point north of Caen through the four-mile gap between Hermanville-sur-Mer and the Canadian sector. During the late morning, however, the British advance had been slowed by a number of factors and by the early afternoon, the Germans had started to exploit the delay in British progress to push the armour of Generalleutnant Edgar Feuchtinger's 21st Panzer Division north past Caen.

When the Allied landings began, this division was disposed with most of its strength south of Caen but with some units on each side of the River Orne between Caen and the sea. The 21st Panzer Division contained many veterans of the North African fighting among its strength of 16,000 men, and its armour included 127 PzKpfw IV medium tanks and 40 assault guns supported by 24 88mm dual-role anti-aircraft/anti-tank guns. From the early morning of 6 June the division's two Panzergrenadier regiments had been given the task of supporting the 736th

Heavily laden infantry of the British 3rd Division on Sword beach.

Grenadier Regiment in its task of eliminating the British 6th Airborne Division's air-head east of the River Orne. The division's two armoured battle groups were then diverted from the British 6th Airborne Division when the German LXXXIV Corps began to appreciate the threat to Caen posed by the British 3rd Infantry Division.

By the time this decision was taken at 0845 hours, some 75 minutes after the beginning of the British seaborne invasion, the 21st Panzer Division was poorly placed to make a decisive intervention, for it was now highly dispersed with its two Panzergrenadier regiments in contact with the British 6th Airborne Division, its anti-aircraft battalion around Caen, its anti-tank guns on Périers ridge with a battalion of field guns to their south, the rest of its artillery on the high ground about 15 miles to the south-east of Caen, and its armour (mainly the 22nd Panzer Regiment) north-east of Falaise.

The German armoured advance was soon detected by air reconnaissance and then attacked by low-flying warplanes: as it started to cross the River Orne at Caen and Colombelles, the 21st Panzer Division had been whittled down to just 90 fighting vehicles. Despite this diminution of the division's armoured strength, the Germans would clearly still be able to attack north and north-west from Caen during the late afternoon or early evening. This threatened to widen the gap between the British 3rd and Canadian 3rd Infantry Divisions.

During the afternoon elements of the 21st Panzer Division were in action between the 185th Infantry Brigade and the Canadians, eventually pushing forward through this gap to reach the sea at Lion-sur-Mer before pulling back when the sight of Allied glider trains raised the spectre of the division's isolation by a landing in its rear. During the afternoon, however, Major General Rennie became worried by the increasing threat along his division's right flank, and therefore decided to cover this flank more strongly. Rennie therefore ordered the 9th Infantry Brigade to locate itself in positions that covered the bridges over the River Orne against a possible German onslaught from the west.

The assembly of the 9th Infantry Brigade was now delayed still further by the arrival on brigade HQ of a German mortar bomb, which severely wounded Brigadier Cunningham and many of his staff. Temporary command passed to the commanding officer of the 2nd RUR, and the 9th Infantry Brigade occupied positions on the high ground between Périers sur le Dan and St Aubin d'Arquenay, just to the west of the main road south to Caen. Here the brigade halted for the night in a westward-facing position between the 8th Brigade to its north and the 185th Brigade to its south and south-east.

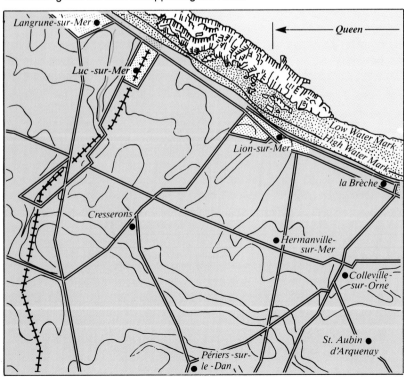

THE BATTLES

153rd Infantry Brigade

The last element of the British I Corps to arrive in Normandy on D-Day was the 153rd Infantry Brigade of the British 51st (Highland) Infantry Division. This was the corps' follow-up division, and had been gathered in Essex for the move to France, which was undertaken from Southend. The brigade was carried to France by Force L together with the fighting elements of the British XXX Corps' British 7th Armoured Division. The preceding convoy had lost a motor transport ship to German coastal artillery fire, but the Force L convoy used smoke and electronic counter-measures to avoid the attentions of the German gunners. The 153rd Infantry Brigade's three infantry battalions arrived during the evening of 6 June, but took no part in the fighting.

The Normandy landings had taken the Germans completely by surprise. Reports of the American and British airborne landings had soon begun to reach the HQs of the relevant German corps (those of LXXXIV and LXXXI Corps, located at St Lô and Rouen respectively) and were then passed to higher HQs, namely those of the Fifteenth and Seventh Armies, then Army Group 'B' and finally OB West (High Command in the West). The commanders of the German Seventh and Fifteenth Armies, Generaloberst Friedrich Dollmann and Generaloberst Hans von Sallmuth, agreed from the start that the Allied operation posed a real threat, but this was not echoed at higher level, where Generalfeldmarschall Gerd von Rundstedt, the OB West, and Generalleutnant Dr. Hans Speidel, chief of staff of Army Group 'B' and deputizing for Generalfeldmarschall Erwin Rommel who was absent in Germany, agreed initially that the landings were a feint. At 0245 hours the Seventh Army gave the LXXXIV Corps its 91st Airlanding Division to help eliminate the US airborne landing, and at 0700 hours the 21st Panzer Division was allocated to the Seventh Army for a similar role against the British airborne landing.

But as the nature and extent of the Allied landings began to make themselves clear, and as local commanders called for additional strength, the confidence of von Rundstedt and Speidel in the accuracy of their initial diagnosis began to waver: what had at first seemed to be an airborne diversion intended to draw German forces away from the real invasion area, probably the Pas-de-Calais, was now becoming clear as a more threatening Allied effort, as indicated by the commitment of major ground forces including armoured and infantry formations. At 0500 hours von Rundstedt ordered Speidel to move SS Gruppenführer Fritz Witt's 12th SS Panzer Division to a position behind the German 711th Grenadier Division for intervention if this became necessary, and to warn the Panzer-Lehr Division of Generalleutnant Fritz Bayerlein's for rapid movement.

These two Panzer divisions were the components of SS Oberstgruppenführer 'Sepp' Dietrich's I SS Panzer Corps, which was the theatre reserve of the Oberkommando der Wehrmacht (OKW, or Armed Forces High Command) under Adolf Hitler's direct supervision. Von Rundstedt's sensible move was then vetoed by the OKW in response to Hitler's belief that the Normandy operation could only be a feint. It was only at 1000 hours that Hitler and the OKW agreed that the 12th SS Panzer and Panzer-Lehr Divisions could be moved and prepared for movement respectively, but that neither was to be committed without OKW's express permission. It was not until 1430 hours that Hitler finally allocated I SS Panzer Corps to OB West, and as a result it was 1700 hours before the corps' two divisions began to move forward as the major combat formations of a strengthened I SS Panzer Corps that was now to include the 21st Panzer and 716th Infantry Divisions to meet 'the desire of the OKW that the enemy in the bridgehead be destroyed by the evening of 6th June as there is a danger of fresh landings by sea and air . . . The bridgehead must be cleared today.' The 12th SS Panzer and Panzer-Lehr Divisions had been too distant to intervene on D-Day, but Hitler's vacillations had compounded the errors of his senior commanders, and it was now a problem of too little and too late.

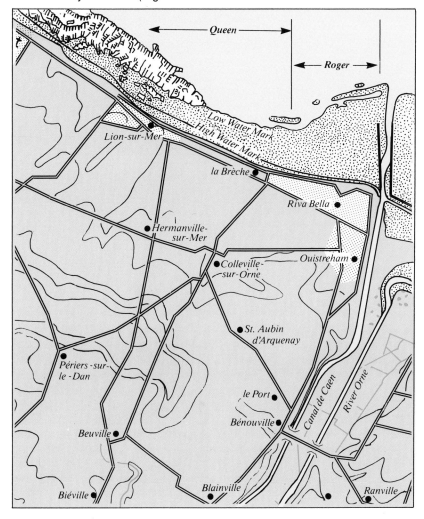

THE BATTLES
1st Special Service Brigade

The task of the 1st Special Service Brigade was to land to the left of the 8th Infantry Brigade and move on Ouistreham to neutralize a battery of German coast-defence guns threatening the British naval forces and other shipping off Sword Beach, and then to link up across the Canal de Caen and River Orne with the British 6th Airborne Division's right-hand units holding the two bridges over these waterways. These primary tasks were complemented by the secondary task of co-operating with the 2nd East Yorkshire of the 8th Infantry Brigade in the provision of a left-hand flank guard for the British 3rd Infantry Division.

The first element of the 1st Special Service Brigade to arrive was No. 4 Commando, which came ashore on Sword Beach and turned east toward Ouistreham in the wake of the 2nd East Yorkshire. This was followed by two French troops of No. 10 (Inter-Allied) Commando and then the brigade's other three Commandos. The opposition was found by elements of Oberst Hafner's 736th Grenadier Regiment of General-leutnant Wilhelm Richter's 716th Infantry Division which had been in action against elements of the British 6th Airborne Division since the early hours of that morning.

Four Centaur tanks of the Royal Marine Armoured Support Regiment gave the commandos very useful support in the capture of the Riva Bella battery. This concrete-casemated position had received a real pasting by bombers and naval guns, but was now found by the victorious commandos to have been stripped of its guns. Farther to the east, men of the 1st Special Service Brigade were supported by 10 vehicles of the 79th Assault Squadron, Royal Engineers, in reaching the mouth of the Canal de Caen. There followed a hard fight for the canal mouth and its lock, resulting in the capture of 60 Germans, and the commandos then discovered that while the lock gates were free of demolition charges, the associated bridge was temporarily unusable as its eastern span had been blown.

With the brigadier's personal piper well to the fore, 1st Special Service Brigade now moved on the bridges over the River Orne, arriving just behind schedule at exactly 1400 hours after advancing nine miles and in the process capturing several German strongpoints and neutralizing a battery of artillery firing on allied shipping. The commandos crossed the river and linked up with the airborne troops at Ranville and le Mariquet, but this British bridgehead was still hard-pressed as the Germans held the higher ground to the south at Hérouvillette and Longueval.

No. 3 Commando was detached to support the airborne troops as No. 6 Commando and No. 45 (Royal Marine) Commandos set off to take Bréville and Merville. The commandos secured Merville but failed to dislodge the Germans from Bréville, which remained a thorn in the British left flank for another week, and the men of the 1st Special Service Brigade ended D-Day in an arc facing north-east between Hauger and le Plein, with a detachment forward of this line at Merville.

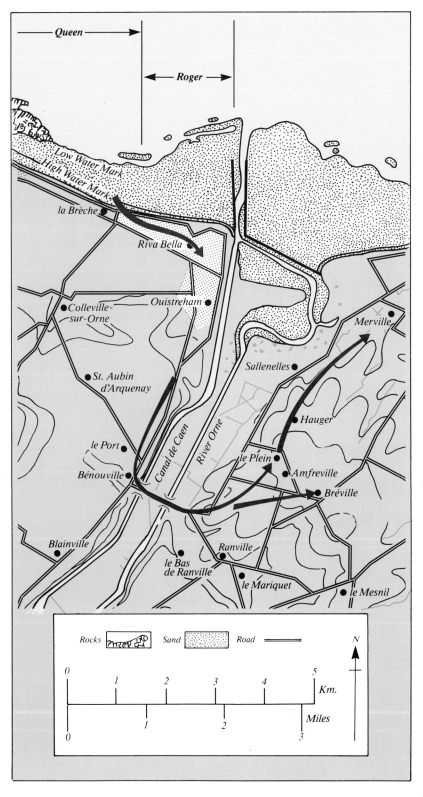

THE BATTLES

4th Special Service Brigade

There was a tactically dangerous gap of some three miles between the eastern end of the Canadian 3rd Infantry Division's landing area at St.-Aubin-sur-Mer and the western end of the British 3rd Infantry Division's landing area at Lion-sur-Mer, and the task of briding this gap fell to the 4th Special Service Brigade. This allocated two of its four Royal Marine Commandos to the task, single commandos being attached to the flanks of the Canadian and British formations. Nos 48 and 41 (Royal Marine) Commandos were thus to come ashore on the left of the Canadian landing and the right of the British landings respectively.

The task of No.41 (Royal Marine) Commando was to link up with the 1st Battalion, The South Lancashire Regiment, which was the right-hand battalion of the 8th Infantry Brigade, and then take the position in Lion-sur-Mer held by elements of Oberst Hafner's 736th Grenadier Regiment.

The primary task of the South Lancashires was the capture of Hermanville-sur-Mer, so it was only a single company of this battalion that moved west to link up with the men of No.41 (Royal Marine) Commando. This had suffered in a difficult landing just to the east of Lion-sur-Mer, where the approaches to the beaches are notably rocky, and too many casualties on the beach.

Once they had established contact with the company of the South Lancashires, the commandos moved west along the coast directly toward Lion-sur-Mer, a potent defensive position whose retention by the Germans prevented any junction between the British and Canadian 3rd Infantry Divisions as its weapons could threaten the right-flank of the British formation.

The German position was well embedded in the centre of this small coastal town, which meant that the commandos had to clear the eastern approaches before they could tackle the strongpoint proper. The commandos lacked armoured support at this stage of their attack, however, so the only way they could come within effective striking distance of the German strongpoint was by means of hand-to-hand fighting through the houses on the eastern outskirts of the town. The commandos made some progress, but they suffered heavy casualties and this inevitably slowed the rate of their advance on the central position.

Eventually the commandos' progress was effectively halted, but at this juncture hope was again raised by the appearance of some armour. This comprised three specialized fighting vehicles of the 5th Engineer Assault Regiment, Royal Engineers. The attack was resumed with these fighting vehicles in the van, but the Germans concentrated the fire of their strongpoint's single piece of artillery on the fighting vehicles. One by one, the Royal Engineers' vehicles were knocked out by the German fire, the attack of the com-

41 Royal Marine Commando come ashore on Sword.

mandos was again halted, and Lion-sur-Mer remained untaken during D-Day.

The position of the Royal Marine Commandos was itself threatened later in the day. The Germans holding the strongpoint in Lion-sur-Mer were in no position to undertake an offensive foray, which would have threatened the strongpoint's security, but during the afternoon of 6 June the advance elements of Generalleutnant Edgar Feuchtinger's 21st Panzer Division began to approach the coast. It was just such an eventuality that the 4th Special Service Brigade was intended to counter, but the sterling defence of the 185th Infantry Brigade along the Périers ridge farther to the south had slowly pushed the German counter-attack to the west, where it moved into the gap between the British and Canadian 3rd Infantry Divisions. Finding less opposition to their front than their flank, the German armour pushed north toward the sea between the strongpoints still held by the 736th Grenadier Regiment at Luc-sur-Mer in the west and Lion-sur-Mer in the east. During the late afternoon the tanks of the 21st Panzer Division continued to probe northward. In the evening, however, British gliderborne reinforcements streamed over the German positions and the German commanders, fearing that another airborne operation near Caen might cut off the 21st Panzer Division, ordered Feuchtinger to pull back: some of his tanks had reached the coast just to the west of Lion-sur-Mer before being called back, but most were between Périers-sur-le-Dan and Anguerny. The division settled in positions extending east from Cambes for the night, and the German tank threat to No.41 (Royal Marine) Commando did not therefore materialize. Badly mauled and much in need of reinforcement, the men of No.41 (Royal Marine) Commando halted for the night in the eastern approaches to Lion-sur-Mer.

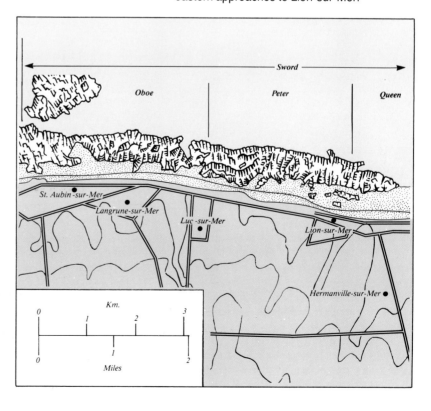

British 6th Airborne Division

In 1940 the British established the Central Landing School at Manchester's Ringway airport to evaluate airborne operations under the aegis of the Director of Combined Operations, but this effort enjoyed only a low priority until Prime Minister Winston Churchill minuted the Chiefs-of-Staff Committee that he wanted to see the creation of a 5,000-man parachute corps without delay. Volunteers of the right calibre were found without difficulty, and progress was made in the development of airborne units and tactics, but the limiting factor was the Royal Air Force's lack of adequate transport and glider-towing aircraft, together with this service's reluctance to see any of its strength diverted to a secondary task, as the RAF saw such operations.

The UK's first operational airborne unit was No. 2 Commando, which became the 11th Special Air Service Battalion (with one parachute wing and one glider wing) during November 1940 and during September 1941 the 1st Battalion, The Parachute Regiment, when it became the first unit to be absorbed into Brigadier R.N. Gale's newly created 1st Parachute Brigade. Two more battalions were soon raised, and in October 1941 Major General F.A.M. Browning was appointed to the new position of Commander, Para-Troops and Airborne Troops. At the same time, an infantry brigade was diverted to become a gliderborne air-landing brigade. By the end of 1941 it was clear that British airborne warfare capabilities merited a new organization, the more so as the Americans had promised large numbers of Douglas C-47 Skytrain transport and glider-towing aircraft that entered British service with the name Dakota. In November of that year Browning was appointed to command of the British 1st Airborne Division.

The formation entrusted with the airborne assault on the left flank of the British assault landing in Operation Overlord was the British 6th Airborne Division commanded by Major General R.N. Gale, who led the division from its creation to 8 December 1944, when he was succeeded by Major General E.L. Bols. The task of the division in Operation Overlord was to land units by parachute and glider in the area to the east of the seaborne landings for the establishment of an air-head whose two primary tasks were the capture of the Canal de Caen and River Orne crossings midway between Caen and Ouistreham, and the provision of a left-flank guard for the seaborne landings against German attacks from the east.

The British 6th Airborne Division had been created on 3 May 1943 with the formation of the divisional headquarters, but the divisional commander assumed command only four days later, and the divisional headquarters was brought up to full establishment only on 23 September 1943. The division's first element was the 6th Airlanding Brigade, which came under command on 6 May 1943, and this was joined later in the

same month by the 3rd Parachute Brigade and the 72nd Independent Infantry Brigade, which arrived on 15 and 28 May respectively. The latter unit remained part of the division for only three days to the end of the month, and was supplanted on 1 June 1943 by the 5th Parachute Brigade, whose HQ was created out of that of the 72nd Independent Infantry Brigade. For the rest of the war the British 6th Airborne Division's units were the 3rd and 5th Parachute Brigades and 6th Airlanding Brigade.

The British 6th Airborne Division served under the GHQ Home Forces from its creation to 3 December 1943, when it passed to control of the HQ Airborne Troops for the period between 4 December 1943 and 5 June 1944. From the next day the British 6th Airborne Division came under the British I Corps for the Normandy campaign, and remained under control of this formation until 30 August 1944, when it passed to the control of the British 21st Army Group before returning to the UK on 3 September 1944 as a part of the British I Airborne Corps from 5 September 1944. Command passed to the War Office on 12 September and then back to the British I Airborne Corps on 1 October 1944. The division returned to North-West Europe on 24 December 1944 under command successively of the British 21st Army Group, British XXX Corps, 21st Army Group, British VIII Corps and finally 21st Army Group. The division saw no action during this period, and returned to the UK and control of the British I Airborne Corps on 24 February 1945. On 19 March 1945 the division was allocated to the US XVIII Airborne Corps, and fought under its command in the first stage of the Rhine battle (23 March – 1 April 1945) before coming under command of the British VIII Corps on 29 March 1945. The division saw no more fighting after the Rhine battle, but reverted to the US XVIII Airborne Corps on 1 May 1945. The division saw out the remaining days of World War II under US control, and reverted to the British I Airborne Corps only on 19 May 1945, when it returned to the UK.

At this point it is illuminating to consider the standard organization of the British airborne division at the time of Operation Overlord. The organization was based on a personnel strength

Major General Richard 'Windy' Gale was a pioneer of British airborne forces, and raised the 1st Parachute Brigade. By 1944 he had risen to command of the British 6th Airborne Division, which he led under very difficult circumstances in Operation Overlord. Though superficially a typical Indian Army officer (he had been born in India and was Master of the Delhi Foxhouds before World War II), Gale was in fact a daring planner who could cause concern by the blunt lucidity of his words but who proved himself capable of infusing his men with the confidence and skills to carry out his plans.

6th AIRBORNE DIVISION
(Major General R.N. Gale)

3rd Parachute Brigade
(Brigadier S.J.L. Hill)

5th Parachute Brigade
(Brigadier J.H.N. Poett)

6th Airlanding Brigade
(Brigadier Hon. H.K.M. Kindersley)

6th Airborne Division – Divisional Troops

of 12,148 all ranks, 6,210 vehicles together with 935 trailers, and weapons that ranged in size from pistols to cruiser tanks. The division's vehicles included 3,269 bicycles (1,907 MKV and 1,362 folding bicycles), 1,233 motorcycles (529 lightweight and 704 solo motorcycles), 1,044 cars (904 5-cwt Jeeps, 115 miscellaneous cars and 25 scout cars), 25 Universal on Bren Carriers, 24 ambulances, 120 15-cwt trucks, 438 3-ton trucks, 26 tractors, and 22 tanks (11 cruiser and 11 light tanks). The weapons included 2,942 pistols, 7,171 Lee Enfield rifles, 6,504 Sten submachine guns, 966 Bren light machine guns, 46 Vickers Mk I medium/heavy machine guns, 535 mortars (474 2-in, 56 3-in and 5 4.2-in weapons), 392 PIAT anti-tank weapons, 23 20mm towed anti-aircraft guns, 38 man-portable flamethrowers, and 127 guns (27 75mm towed pack howitzers, 84 towed 6-pounder anti-tank guns and 16 towed 17-pounder anti-tank guns).

Divisional command was exercised from the Divisional HQ, where the divisional commander and his staff enjoyed the support of several types of specialist as well as the Airborne Divisional HQ Defence Platoon, the Divisional Field

Security Section and an independent parachute company. The Divisional HQ controlled the formation's three brigades (two parachute and one airlanding) and the organic divisional troops. Each brigade was based on a Brigade HQ with its own Brigade HQ Defence Platoon and three battalions. The three battalions were the fighting strength of the brigade. In the parachute brigades, each battalion had a strength of 29 officers and 584 other ranks in one HQ company and three rifle companies. The HQ company had five platoons, two of them each equipped with four 3-in mortars and one with 10 PIATs. Each rifle company had three platoons. In the glider-borne airlanding brigade, each battalion had a strength of 47 officers and 817 other ranks in one support company, one anti-aircraft/anti-tank company and four rifle companies. The support company had six platoons including one with four 3-in mortars. The anti-aircraft/anti-tank company had four platoons including two with 12 20mm AA guns and the other two with eight 6-pounder anti-tank guns. Each rifle company had four platoons. It should also be noted that the gliders used for the delivery of the airlanding brigade were operated by wings whose varying number of squadrons each had a varying number of flights each with 20 gliders. Each glider was flown by two men of The Glider Pilot Regiment, who were trained to fight alongside the men of the airlanding brigade.

The capability of the parachute and airlanding brigades was greatly bolstered by the divisional troops controlled by Divisional HQ. The Royal Armoured Corps provided an airborne armoured reconnaissance regiment. The Royal Artillery provided an HQ Airborne Division RA controlling one airlanding light regiment and one airlanding anti-tank regiment. The Royal Engineers provided a HQ Airborne Division RE controlling two parachute engineer squadrons and one airborne field company. The Royal Signals provided an Airborne Divisional Signals unit. The Royal Army Service Corps provided an HQ Airborne Division RASC controlling one airborne light company and two airborne light divisional companies. The Royal Army Medical Corps provided two parachute field ambulances and one airlanding field ambulance. The Royal Army Ordnance Corps provided one airborne divisional ordnance field park. The Royal Electrical and Mechanical Engineers provided an HQ Airborne Division REME controlling one airborne divisional workshop, one armoured Airlanding Light Aid Detachment 'Type A', one unarmoured Airlanding Light Aid Detachment 'Type A', four Airlanding Light Aid Detachments 'Type B' and one Airlanding Light Aid Detachment 'Type C'. And the Corps of Military Police provided an airborne divisional provost company. The organic troops were completed by an airborne divisional postal unit, a mobile photo enlargement centre and a forward observer unit.

HQ 6th Airborne Division

Royal Armoured Corps
6th Airborne Armoured Reconnaissance Regiment

Royal Artillery
211th Battery, 53rd Airlanding Light Regiment
3rd and 4th Airlanding Attack Batteries [arrived by sea]

Royal Engineers
3rd and 591st Parachute Squadrons
249th Field Company (Airborne) [arrived by sea]

Royal Signals
6th Airborne Divisional Signals

Infantry
22nd Independent Parachute Company [to prepare dropping and landing zones]

Army Air Corps
Nos 1 and 2 Wings, The Glider Pilot Regiment

Royal Army Medical Corps
224th and 225th Parachute Field Ambulances
195th Airlanding Field Ambulance

Royal Army Service Corps
716th Light Composite Company
398th Composite Company [arrived by sea]

Royal Electrical and Mechanical Engineers
6th Airborne Divisional Workshop
[of which a strong detachment was landed by glider at H+4 hours]

3rd Parachute Brigade

The 3rd Parachute Brigade came into existence in the UK during 7 November 1942 when the brigade HQ was created out of the 223rd Independent Infantry Brigade's HQ under Brigadier Sir A.B.G. Stanier, Bart. At the time of its creation, the 3rd Parachute Brigade had just two battalions of The Parachute Regiment, namely the 7th (Light Infantry) and 8th (Midland Counties) Battalions, but these were supplemented from 5 December 1942 by the 9th (Home Counties) Battalion. On 8 August 1943, the brigade lost the 7th (Light Infantry) Battalion, but a full three-battalion strength was restored just three days later when the brigade received the Canadian 1st Parachute Battalion on 11 August.

Stanier was succeeded in command on 8 December 1942 by Brigadier G.W. Lathbury, and later commanders were Lieutenant Colonel S.J.L. Hill (acting) from 25 April 1943, Brigadier E.W.C. Flavell from 4 May 1943, and Brigadier

The Parachute Regiment

S.J.L. Hill from 2 June 1943. Hill led the brigade in Normandy, and later commanders were Colonel R.G. Parker (acting) from 20 December 1944 and Hill once more from 30 December 1944.

The brigade was under War Office command at the time of its creation, but only one week later was allocated to the British 1st Airborne Division on 13 November 1942. The brigade stayed with this parent formation until 11 April 1943, when it was again taken under War Office control before being reallocated to the British 6th Airborne Division on 15 May 1943, and the brigade remained part of this division for the rest of World War II. The brigade fought in the Normandy landing on 6 June 1944, and its only other battle in World War II was the Rhine (23 March – 1 April 1945).

In Operation Overlord, the 3rd Parachute Brigade was given the twin tasks of isolating the Allied lodgement area against the possibility of German counter-attack from the east (by destroying the bridges over the River Dives at Troarn, Bures, Robehomme and Varaville, and by blocking all German access routes from the south-east), and of eliminating within one hour the threat of the Merville battery whose powerful 150mm guns would otherwise be able to enfilade the Allied naval forces carrying out and supporting the seaborne invasion. After destroying the Dives river bridges, the battalions involved were to fall back towards the River Orne and occupy blocking positions.

3rd PARACHUTE BRIGADE
(Brigadier S.J.L. Hill)

8th Battalion, The Parachute Regiment
9th Battalion, The Parachute Regiment
1st Battalion, The Canadian Parachute Regiment

5th Parachute Brigade

The 5th Parachute Brigade came into existence in the UK during 1 June 1942 when the brigade HQ was created out of the 72nd Independent Infantry Brigade's HQ under the command of Brigadier E.W.C. Flavell. At the time of its creation, the 5th Parachute Brigade had just two battalions of The Parachute Regiment, namely the 12th and 13th Battalions, but these were supplemented from 9 August 1943 by the 7th (Light Infantry) Battalion. These three battalions continued to constitute the 5th Parachute Brigade for the rest of the war.

Flavell was succeeded in command on 5 July 1943 by Brigadier J.H.N. Poett, and this officer remained in command of the 5th Parachute Brigade for the rest of the war. Poett thus commanded in Normandy, where the 5th Parachute Brigade received its baptism of fire. The brigade was a component of the British 6th Airborne Division from the time of its creation to the end

The Parachute Regiment

of the war in Europe, and on 20 July 1945 was revised as the 5th Parachute Brigade Group for service against the Japanese. The brigade group retained its three parachute infantry battalions but was reinforced with the 4th Airlanding Anti-tank Battery, RA, the 3rd Airborne Squadron and Detachment 286 Field Park Squadron, RE, the 22nd Independent Parachute Company, AAC, the Parachute Platoon of the 716th Light Composite Company, RASC, and the 225th Parachute Field Ambulance, RAMC. The brigade HQ moved to India by air between 20 and 28 July 1945, and the other elements followed by sea so that the brigade was able to concentrate once more in the middle of August 1945. Japan surrendered before the brigade saw action in the Far East.

Thus the 5th Parachute Brigade's only fighting was seen in the European theatre, where the brigade fought in the Normandy landing on 6 June 1944, and then in the Rhine battle (23 March – 1 April 1945).

In Operation Overlord, the 5th Parachute Brigade was given the task of taking and holding the bridges over the Canal de Caen and the River Orne north-west of Ranville. The parachute battalions would land and seize the bridges before these could be blown by the Germans, and then clear the landing zones on which gliders could land to deliver the reinforcements and heavy equipment (including weapons) that would strengthen the defence of the bridgehead.

5th PARACHUTE BRIGADE
(Brigadier J.H.N. Poett)

7th Battalion, The Parachute Regiment
12th Battalion, The Parachute Regiment
13th Battalion, The Parachute Regiment

6th Airlanding Brigade

The 6th Airlanding Brigade came into existence in the UK during 6 May 1943, and its first commander was Colonel A.M. Toye (acting), who arrived on 14 May 1943 and was succeeded just 10 days later, on 24 May 1943 by Brigadier Hon. H.K.M. Kindersley. At the time of its creation, the 6th Airlanding Brigade had no battalions under command, the first two of its three units arriving on 16 May 1943 in the form of the 2nd Battalion, The Oxfordshire and Buckinghamshire Light Infantry and the 1st Battalion, The Royal Ulster Rifles. The brigade's last unit was the 12th Battalion, The Devonshire Regiment, which arrived on 30 July 1943.

Kindersley retained command of the 6th Airlanding Brigade until 12 June 1944, when he was wounded and replaced by Colonel R.G. Parker (acting) until the arrival of Brigadier E.W.C. Flavell on 15 June 1944. Flavell remained in

**The Oxfordshire &
Buckinghamshire
Light Infantry**

command to 19 January 1945, when he was succeeded by Brigadier R.H. Bellamy, who remained in command of the brigade for the rest of the war.

The brigade was part of the British 6th Airborne Division from the time of its creation to the end of World War II. The brigade fought in the Normandy landing on 6 June 1944, and its only other battle in World War II was the Rhine (23 March – 1 April 1945). The brigade was thus in North-West Europe to 3 September 1944, when it returned to the UK until 23 December 1944. It then moved back to North-West Europe, where it remained for the rest of the war with the exception of the one-month period between 24 February and 24 March 1945.

In Operation Overlord, the 6th Airlanding Brigade was given the vital task of supporting the two parachute brigades, most notably the 5th Parachute Brigade of the British 6th Airborne Division. For this task two of the brigade's battalions, the 2nd Oxfordshire and Buckinghamshire and the 1st Royal Ulster Rifles, together with one company of the Devons, were to be landed in the early evening by Airspeed Horsa glider. With the aid of specialized heavy equipment delivered by General Aircraft Hamilcar gliders, the airlanding infantry units were to reinforce the parachute battalions and hold off the Germans until the units of the airborne division were relieved by units arriving from the seaborne lodgement.

6th AIRLANDING BRIGADE
(Brigadier Hon. H.K.M. Kindersley)

2nd Battalion, The Oxfordshire and Buckinghamshire Light Infantry
1st Battalion, The Royal Ulster Rifles
A Company of the 12th Battalion, The Devonshire Regiment
[other companies arrived by sea on D+1]

Coup-de-Main Special Force

The *Coup-de-Main* Special Force was created from elements of the 6th Airlanding Brigade and the 6th Airborne Division's organic divisional troops for a very special task whose failure could signal disaster for the British 6th Airborne Division. The task was made necessary by the geography of the area allocated to the British I Corps in Operation Overlord: this was to involve the seaborne landing of the Canadian 3rd and British 3rd Infantry Divisions between la Rivière and Ouistreham with the primary objective of taking Caen, and the airborne landing of the British 6th Airborne Division east of Ouistreham to protect the left flank of the seaborne assault and provide room for the lodgement to be extended east and south of Caen. But the seaborne and airborne elements of the British I Corps' assault were divided by the Canal de Caen and

The Royal Ulster Rifles

The Devonshire Regiment

River Orne, waterways running roughly parallel to each other between Caen and the English Channel at Ouistreham.

It was appreciated that the airborne units, smaller and considerably more lightly equipped than their conventional counterparts, could not long survive the type of counter-attack the Germans would inevitably launch against their air-head to the east of the River Orne. So speedy relief was essential before German reinforcement, especially of armour, arrived. This relief had to cross the Canal de Caen and River Orne, so it was vital that the road link across the canal and river between Ranville and Bénouville should be taken and held, together with its two bridges.

This was the task of the *Coup-de-Main* Special Force under Major R.L. Howard. The force was to comprise two parties, each of three platoons with engineer support, carried in six gliders. These were to be released over the coast at an altitude of 5,000ft and then fly to the bridges, where they were to land as close as possible to their targets. The infantry were then to storm the German bridge defences and secure the approaches from each direction as the engineers checked for demolition charges and defused any that they found. The two parties were then to hold out against any and all German counter-attack until relieved by men of the parachute battalions from the east and/or units advancing from the coast.

COUP-DE-MAIN SPECIAL FORCE
(Major R.J. Howard)

**two platoons of B Company of the 2nd Battalion,
  The Oxfordshire and Buckinghamshire Light Infantry
D Company of the 2nd Battalion,
  The Oxfordshire and Buckinghamshire Light Infantry
detachment of the 249th Field Company (Airborne), Royal Engineers**

THE BATTLES

3rd Parachute Brigade

Of the three drop zones fixed for the British 6th Airborne Division, two were allocated to the 3rd Parachute Brigade, which had two British and one Canadian parachute battalions and, for its specialized demolition tasks, the 3rd Parachute Squadron of the Royal Engineers.

The drop zones allocated to the brigade were 'K' west of Touffreville and 'V' west of Varaville, and the arrival of the brigade on these zones was to take place in three waves: the first would arrive at 0020 hours on 6 June and would be small, comprising basically the pathfinder and other advanced elements, the second would arrive between 0045 and 0105 hours and comprise most of the brigade's men, and the third would arrive at 0320 hours and comprise the brigade's heavier equipment such as anti-tank guns, bulldozers, Jeeps, engineering equipment and stores.

The operations of the 3rd Parachute Brigade were hampered by bad drops whose effects were worsened by the fact that Brigadier Hill, his staff and parts of the 1st and 9th Battalions landed some 1,000 yards too far to the east of the 'V' drop zone in the area of the flooded River Dives and had then walked into the target area of a heavy bombing attack, with the result that a number of men, including the brigadier, were wounded: it was dusk before these command elements reached the rest of the brigade. The bad drop resulted mainly from the last bomber attack on the Merville battery, which had thrown up masses of dust and smoke that had drifted south on the north wind and obscured the marker lights on the drop zones.

The 8th Parachute Battalion had a poor drop in the southern 'K' zone, and moved to destroy the bridges at Troarn and Bures before pulling back to the north-west for its secondary task of consolidating in the woods near Bavent, which it was to hold until relieved. The Canadian 1st Parachute Battalion was widely scattered round the northern 'V' zone, and was tasked with the destruction of the bridges at Varaville and Robehomme. In both zones, the senior available officer of each battalion was now faced with the problem of assembling what men and equipment came to hand without undue delay, and then of moving off toward the objectives in the belief that speed was of the essence and that their meagre numbers would be swelled during the day as stragglers found their parent battalions.

The wounded commander of the 8th Parachute Battalion was faced with the problem that an error had resulted in half of his pathfinder and advance party, together with some of his second-wave force, landing on the division's third drop zone, known as 'N' and located three miles to the north. There was also considerable dispersion on the 'K' zone. Here a party of only 160 men

assembled, and the battalion commander decided that he lacked the strength to tackle Troarn and that his only sensible course was therefore to group his available strength on the high ground to the south-west of the Bavent woods, where it could cover the group attacking the Bures bridge.

Meanwhile the men who had landed wrongly on the 'N' drop zone had grouped into two parties: one had about 60 paratroops under the battalion mortar officer, and the other about 60 sappers and 25 paratroops under Major J.C.A. Roseveare, RE. Roseveare's party had a Jeep and trailer loaded with medical stores, and nearly 500 lb of explosive and demolition equipment on six trolleys. The two parties headed for their original objectives, and met to the west of the Bavent woods. Here most of the paratroops were

left to establish a solid base, while Roseveare divided his sappers into two groups. The larger was sent with most of the demolition equipment to blow the bridge at Bures, while Roseveare and eight other men packed themselves and some demolition equipment into the Jeep and trailer before heading for Troarn.

The trolley party pushed through to Bures and blew the bridge over the River Dives much as planned. The small Jeep and trailer party got to Troarn unmolested, but then had to waste 20 minutes cutting through a wire barrier in front of the railway level crossing just west of the village, and then raced through the alerted garrison and down the hill to the river with all guns blazing, in the process losing the Bren gunner on the trailer. Once at the river, the party blew one of the bridge's spans and, ditching the Jeep, moved north on foot.

The surviving eight men had to cross several streams, but managed to link up with the demolition party at Bures before falling back toward the Bavent woods, where they joined forces with the slowly gathering strength of the 8th Parachute Battalion, which had arranged a dusk rendezvous at le Mesnil before taking up positions on the ridge to the west of the Bavent woods.

Farther to the north, the Canadian 1st Parachute Battalion also suffered a widely dispersed arrival and lost a number of men as well as much of its equipment in the flooded River Dives. Even so, the battalion managed to gather sufficient strength to fulfil its tasks. One company reached the bridge at Varaville, which was blown by the attached sappers of the 3rd Parachute Squadron. The Canadians also attacked the Germans' local HQ, which was located in a château protected by a 75mm gun in a pillbox surrounded by weapon pits inside a mined barbed-wire perimeter. It was only after daybreak that the Canadians had taken most of their objectives, and late morning before the survivors managed to break away. At Robehomme, the bridge was destroyed by a smaller party of 60 Canadian paratroops, who managed to assemble enough explosives to achieve their end under supervision by a Royal Engineer officer whose men and equipment had not arrived.

The most daunting task facing the 3rd Parachute Brigade was that entrusted to its third unit, Lieutenant Colonel T. Otway's 9th Parachute Battalion: the destruction of the Merville battery, thought to contain four 150mm guns capable of inflicting serious damage on the invasion fleet and comparatively impervious to destruction by bombers as the guns were in steel-doored concrete casemates 78 in thick covered, in the case of two of them, by an outer layer of earth some 12 ft thick. The whole battery position was protected by mines, wire entanglements, antiaircraft guns, machine guns, weapon pits and an incomplete anti-tank ditch as shown in the accompanying map.

The attack on the Merville Battery.

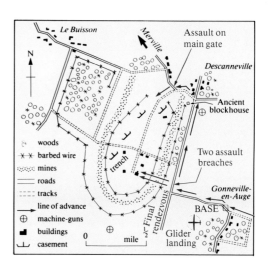

The attack was entrusted to three paratroop companies – one to hold a base position, one to break into the battery, and one to make the final assault with the support of a party that was to crash-land on the battery in gliders. One of the gliders broke its tow over England, and the other two failed to find the battery.

The battalion's drop was widely scattered, and by 0330 hours Otway had gathered only 150 men. There were no assault engineers or specialized equipment, and the only heavy weapons available to Otway's party were one Vickers machine gun and 20 Bangalore torpedoes. The reconnaissance party had reached the battery and marked paths through the outer wire and minefield, and this greatly aided the main party. The advance toward the battery was covered by the men in one of the two *coup-de-main* gliders, who checked the Germans pursuing Otway's party. Otway now revised his tactics and divided his men into three groups: one was to make a diversion while the other two, with the Bangalore torpedoes, broke through the German perimeter and destroyed the guns. Despite an enfilading crossfire from six German machine guns, the paratroops succeeded under exceptionally difficult circumstances and used 'Gammon' charges to destroy the guns, which were found to be just 75mm 'popguns'. The charges detonated at 0500 hours, just 30 minutes before Otway's deadline and at the cost of 75 casualties.

Supported by a party of the Canadian 1st Parachute Battalion, the 80 survivors of the Merville assault now set off for the high ground at le Plein, where the battalion was to become the left-hand element of the 3rd Parachute Brigade's delaying position in an eastward-facing arc extending from le Plein round the front of le Mesnil to a point just north-east of Touffreville. Here the brigade was to have been relieved by elements of the British 3rd Infantry Division, but so far only the 1st Special Service Brigade had moved across the River Orne and perhaps just 2,800 out of an initial 4,800 men of the British 6th Airborne Division's two parachute brigades were thus faced with the prospect of a German counterattack before they could be relieved.

5th Parachute Brigade

The main part of the 5th Parachute Brigade's three battalions and attached 591st Parachute Squadron, RE and 286th Field Park Company, RASC were delivered by 129 aircraft to the 'N' drop zone, and all but five aircraft had completed their drops within 30 minutes of the designated start time.

By 0130 hours the 7th Parachute Battalion had mustered some half of its men together with part of the 591st Parachute Squadron, and the senior officer decided to lose no further time before moving off to undertake its allotted tasks (the reinforcement of the *coup-de-main* party on the bridges over the Canal de Caen and River Orne, even though this meant abandoning all unlocated equipment such as machine guns, mortars and radios. The men quickly reached the bridges and moved over them to reinforce the small *coup-de-main* party holding the western end and then to extend the area of British control at the western end. There was confused, virtually nonstop and extremely bitter fighting between the men of the 7th Parachute Battalion and elements of three German regiments through the early morning in the area of Bénouville and le Pont, and at one point the aid post was overrun. At daybreak the paratroops had yielded no ground, however, and the fighting continued unabated. In Bénouville one British company was engaged on three sides but managed to hold its position with the aid of the battalion's machine gunners and mortar men, who lacked their own weapons and now joined in the fray with weapons taken from the dead. Matters were still extremely precarious for the battalion, but from the north came the sound of heavy fighting, so the paratroops held on and watched for the relief promised by the leading units from the seaborne assault. In fact it was 1400 hours before the leading elements of the 1st Special Service Brigade arrived to relieve the airborne troops on the western end of the bridges. By this time the airborne troops had held their objective for 12 hours against determined German attacks.

The 12th Parachute Battalion enjoyed the advantage of a slightly better drop: 15 of the aircraft made their deliveries accurately and another seven within one mile of the allocated area, but the remaining 10 were well wide of the mark. The battalion's task was to hold the approaches to the waterway bridges from the east. By 0400 hours the battalion had secured the western approaches to the bridges and fanned out as far to the south as le Bas de Ranville. But the battalion's forward elements were outnumbered by some 20 to 1 and faced by German 88mm dual-role anti-aircraft and anti-tank guns firing at pointblank ranges as short as 70 yards. The British had only one 6-pounder gun, and this was useless as its breech had been

Parachute Regiment CMPs guard the cross roads outside Ranville.

broken during the landing. The situation was critical, especially as Generalleutnant Edgar Feuchtinger had on his own initiative sent an armoured battle group of his 21st Panzer Division to support the division's two Panzergrenadier regiments against the paratroops. But luck played into the hands of the British, for at mid-morning Feuchtinger was ordered to turn back the armoured group in preparation for an attack on the British 3rd Infantry Division.

Even so, close-quarter fighting continued with heavy losses on each side. Feuchtinger was later ordered to pull back his Panzergrenadier regiments, but could not comply as the regiments were too closely engaged with the paratroops.

The 13th Parachute Battalion was to take and secure Ranville, and also to work with the RE and RASC elements to protect the 'N' drop zone, and to clear and improve its landing strips. The bulk of the battalion was used to achieve the first of these objectives by 0400 hours. One company of paratroops worked with the RE and RASC elements to clear stakes and mines on the landing strips that were required for the third wave of airborne troops, who began to arrive at 0330 hours in 68 Airspeed Horsa gliders, of which 50 arrived safely. These delivered Major General Gale, much of his HQ staff, heavy engineer stores and the 4th Airlanding Anti-tank Battery, RA, with 11 desperately needed anti-tank guns.

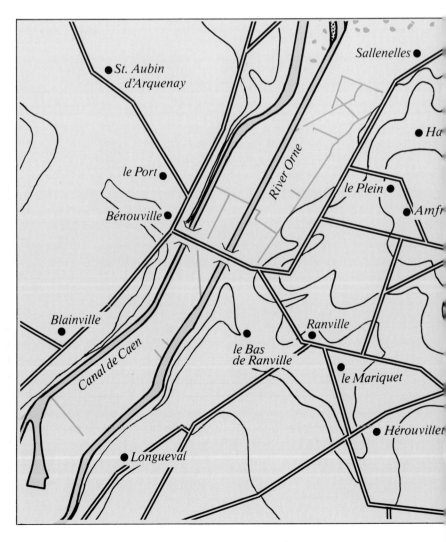

THE BATTLES

6th Airlanding Brigade

The problem faced by all paratroops is the dispersed nature of their arrival on the ground as a result of the delayed sequence in which they exit their aircraft and the vagaries of the air currents through which they must then float. In operation Overlord these basic problems were compounded by the single jump door of the Douglas Dakota paratroop transport, the fact that the men were more heavily loaded than they had been in training and therefore exited more slowly than had been planned, the imprecise navigational accuracy of many Royal Air Force pilots in this nocturnal delivery, and the landed paratroops' difficulty in recovering their equipment and effecting a rendezvous. The result was that many units went off to battle from the drop zones with less than half their men and often with little or no heavy equipment.

This mattered comparatively little at the start of operations, for the paratroops relied on surprise and speed for the attainment of their initial objectives. Where the lack of manpower and equipment became crucial, however, was in the holding of an objective once it had been captured. The

Empty Horsa gliders of the 6th Airlanding Brigade at Ranville after the D-Day landings.

Germans inevitably responded in large numbers with heavy weapons: sustained attacks soon whittled away the paratroops' already depleted numbers, man-carried supplies of small arms ammunition were soon seriously depleted, and the paratroop's ability to fight back was severely curtailed by lack of heavy weapons such as the machine guns and mortars abandoned in the aftermath of a dispersed drop.

This factor was appreciated early in British planning for an airborne capability, and was the reason for the combination of parachute and airlanding brigades in the airborne division. The parachute brigade was based on three small battalions with personal weapons and only a small complement of slightly heavier weapons. The gliderborne airlanding brigade was based on three larger battalions, and thus had greater basic strength as well as a larger complement of heavier weapons and the capacity to arrive with more vehicles and equipment: this brigade therefore offered the capability for more sustained operations.

The British decided on an airborne division with two parachute brigades supported by one airlanding brigade and divisional troops which would be landed mostly by glider together with their specialist equipment. This arrangement was designed for tactical surprise, when the parachute brigades landed without much warning and moved to take their objectives before the enemy could react in strength, and then the capacity for a modestly sustained engagement once the more potent airlanding brigade and the heavier weapons had arrived to bolster the parachute brigades. Even assuming that all the men of the parachute and airlanding brigades arrived safely and rendezvoused as arranged, which was a highly unlikely eventuality, the airborne division would still be weaker than most of the opponents it would be called on to face. The airlanding brigade was only a palliative to the airborne division's inability to fight a sustained battle, so speedy relief or reinforcement by conventional ground formations was more than essential.

The airlanding component of the British 6th Airborne Division in Operation Overlord was the 6th Airlanding Brigade, which was to arrive with two battalions rather than its full three-battalion establishment: the 2nd Battalion, The Oxfordshire and Buckinghamshire Light Infantry was weakened by the removal of one and one-half companies for the *Coup-de-Main* Special Force, and this shortfall in the brigade's gliderborne strength was remedied by the addition of one company of the 12th Battalion, The Devonshire Regiment. The rest of the battalion was to arrive by sea on D+1 together with about half of the organic divisional troops.

The 6th Airlanding Brigade started to arrive in the air-head of the British 6th Airborne Division during the afternoon, effectively doubling the division's manpower strength. The division's fighting strength was also increased by the arrival in other gliders, also on the Main LZ, of the

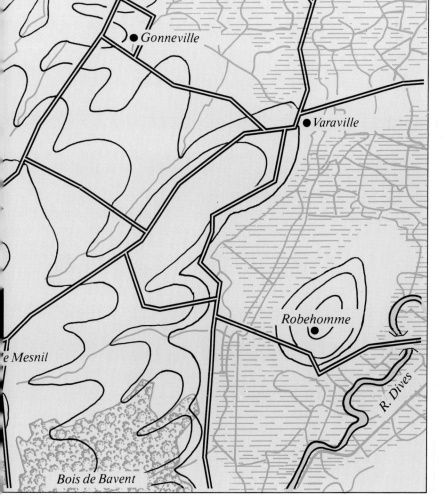

6th Airborne Armoured Reconnaissance Regiment with its light tanks and Jeeps, and of the 211th Battery of the 53rd Airlanding Light Regiment and the 3rd Airlanding Anti-tank Regiment with their light artillery and anti-tank equipments. Much needed ammunition was also included in the 600 containers of equipment and stores that were also parachuted into the air-head at the same time, and further support came with the arrival of medical and supply units.

The men of the 1st Special Service Brigade had already moved over the secured bridges to reinforce the 5th Parachute Brigade (No.3 Commando between le Bas de Ranville and le Mariquet) against German attacks from Longueval and Hérouvillette, and the 3rd Parachute Brigade (Nos 6 and 45 [RM] Commandos) in the direction of Bréville and Merville. The 6th Airlanding Brigade's two battalions moved onto the left flank of the 5th Parachute Brigade south of le Mariquet in preparation for an attack on Hérouvillette and Escoville at dawn on the following day.

As the fighting subsided in the evening of 6 June, the 5th Parachute Brigade was grouped to the south of le Bas de Ranville, the 6th Airlanding Brigade south of le Mariquet, and the more scattered 3rd Parachute Brigade with its 8th Parachute Battalion in the south-east toward Touffreville and Troarn, its Canadian 1st Parachute Battalion in the east around the crossroads at le Mesnil, and its 9th Parachute Battalion in the north-east occupying a more precarious position round le Plein and Hauger separated from the Canadian 1st Parachute Battalion by the continued German presence in Bréville, which was to be a problem for the Allies over the next week, when there was still much serious and bloody fighting to be undertaken.

The *Coup de Main* force between the Caen canal and Orne river bridges.

THE BATTLES

Coup de Main Special Force

Because the only real physical link between the air-head of the British 6th Airborne Division and the seaborne lodgement of the British 3rd Infantry Division was constituted by the twin bridges over the parallel Canal de Caen and River Orne waterways, it was vital that these structures be seized and held against German counterattack. The task was given to Major R.J. Howard's *Coup-de-Main* Special Force of six platoons of the 2nd Battalion, The Oxfordshire and Buckinghamshire Light Infantry, together with a 30-man party of the Royal Engineers' 249th Field Company (Airborne).

The six Airspeed Horsa gliders carrying the force dropped their tows a few minutes after midnight. The first three gliders landed exactly according to plan: one stopped with its nose in the wire round the German defensive position covering the Bénouville bridge and the other two arrived within 100 yards of it. The men of the first two British platoons rushed out of their gliders and stormed this western bridge over the Canal de Caen. The Germans were alert, and of the leading platoon commanders one was killed and the other wounded. Howard then committed his third platoon and the Germans were soon overwhelmed in a sharp firefight, whereupon Howard established his own positions and settled down to await relief.

Of the other three gliders, one landed five miles to the east and its men played no part in this part of the British 6th Airborne Division's operation. The other two landed 100 and 700 yards from their target, the Ranville bridge over the more easterly River Orne. The Germans were not as alert as their partners on the Bénouville bridge, and the two platoons secured the bridge without problem. Within 15 minutes both bridges were thus in British hands, and the sappers were able to confirm that neither structure was mined for demolition.

So far the operation had proceeded with speed and remarkable smoothness, but now the force's task was to hold the bridges until reinforced in the shorter term by the 7th Parachute Battalion from the east, and then relieved in the longer term by the 1st Special Service Brigade from the west. The Germans still held Bénouville and Ranville, and soon heavy fire was directed at the British positions as three tanks approached but then pulled back after the first had been set alight by a PIAT projectile.

Reinforcement came in the form of the 7th Parachute Battalion, which arrived at 0300 hours at about half-strength under Lieutenant Colonel G. Pine-Coffin. The Germans were now preparing a major effort, and severe fighting raged round the bridges until the early afternoon and the arrival of No.46 Commando.

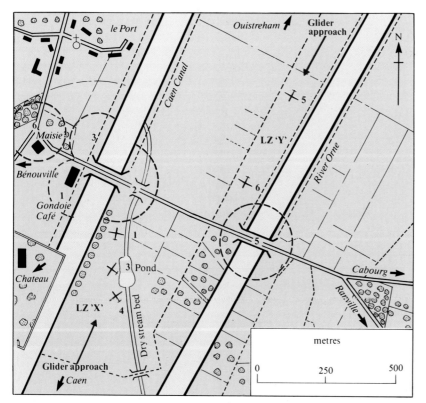

Allied Air Support

The effective use of air power was vital to the success of Operation Overlord. This applied to the period leading to the start of the operation as well as the landings proper and the inland development of the Allied lodgement, and the fact was reflected in the appointment of Air Chief Marshal Sir Arthur Tedder as General Dwight D. Eisenhower's deputy.

The strategic air forces in Europe put at Eisenhower's disposal for the approach to D-Day were commanded by Lieutenant General Carl A. Spaatz, and were Air Chief Marshal Sir Arthur Harris' RAF Bomber Command, Lieutenant General James H. Doolittle's US Eighth Army Air Force and Lieutenant General Nathan F. Twining's US Fifteenth Army Air Force. These were to be used to supplement the tactical efforts of Eisenhower's Allied Expeditionary Air Forces based in England under the command of the Overlord air commander, Air Chief Marshal Sir Trafford Leigh-Mallory.

The AEAF comprised Air Marshal Sir Arthur Coningham's British Second Tactical Air Force and Major General Hoyt S. Vandenburg's US Ninth Army Air Force. From January 1944 onwards these combined air armadas concentrated on targets in occupied Europe with emphasis, in order of priority, upon aircraft production, railways, V-1 sites and airfields in January; V-1 sites, airfields and railways in February; railways, aircraft production, V-1 sites, coastal fortifications and airfields in March; railways, airfields, V-1 sites, coastal fortifications and shipping in April; and railways, rolling stock, road bridges, coastal radar installations, V-1 sites and coastal fortifications in May.

Below: **Well over 50 airfields in the United Kingdom were used to support the D-Day operations.**

The object of this campaign was to halt the movement of German reserves, cut German lines of communication, to destroy the V-1 sites which the Allies believed could threaten the landings, eliminate German aircraft and air facilities in France and the Low Countries, and destroy the coastal radars and fortifications that might warn of the invasion and then severely damage the assault forces at sea.

So successful was this campaign that on 6 June Generalfeldmarschall Hugo Sperree's Luftflotte III had a mere 420 aircraft in northern France to pit against an Allied aerial armada of 10,521 warplanes (3,467 four-engined bombers, 1,645 twin-engined bombers and 5,409 single-engined fighters and fighter-bombers), 2,355 transport aircraft and 867 gliders.

This meant that the Allies had total air superiority. After the beach defences and other targets had been given a last pounding by the heavy bombers, the primary air burden fell to the tactical air forces. Air cover was provided for the ships in the English Channel, the transport of airborne forces, the landing beaches and the pushes toward Caen and Bayeux. The Second Tactical Air Force flew more than 2,000 sorties in 100 operations to attack army HQs, strongpoints, artillery batteries, road junctions, troops, and vehicles. It used aircraft such as the de Havilland Mosquito, Douglas Boston and North American Mitchell bombers, North American Mustang and Supermarine Spitfire fighter-bombers, and Hawker Typhoon attack fighters. Further air activity was undertaken by photo-reconnaissance aircraft. Yet such was the Allies' mastery of the air that over the British sector in this 24-hour period only 36 German aircraft were seen, and of these seven were recorded as destroyed and another three as damaged.

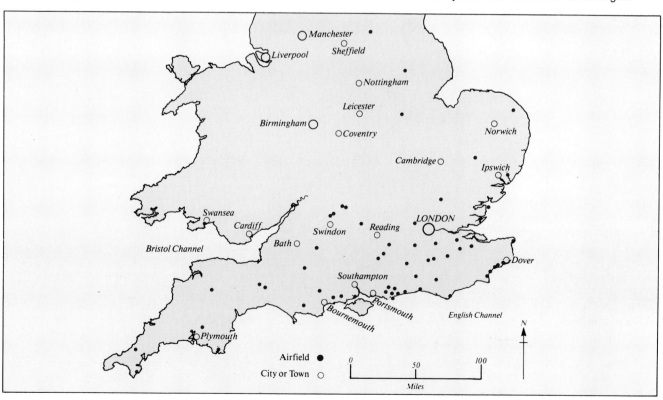

Allied Naval Support

The Allied naval effort in support of the Normandy landings was Operation Neptune, which was planned by the staff Admiral Sir Bertram Ramsay, the Naval Commander-in-Chief Expeditionary Force.

Within the context of the Allied plan to land five infantry divisions (two American in the west and a combination of one Canadian and two British in the east), two task forces were created: Western Naval Task Force under Rear Admiral A.G. Kirk was allocated to the US landings, and the Eastern Naval Task Force under Rear Admiral Sir Philip Vian, flying his flag in the cruiser *Scylla*, was allocated to the Anglo-Canadian landings. For their tasks the two Allied naval commanders each had very substantial naval and assault landing assets.

The Eastern Naval Task Force had four landing ships headquarters, 37 landing ships infantry, three landing ships dock, 408 landing craft assault, 11 landing craft headquarters, 155 landing craft infantry (25 of them American), 130 landing ships tank (37 of them American), 487 landing craft tank, 19 landing craft flak, 16 landing craft gun, 83 landing craft support, 22 landing craft tank (rocket), 100 landing craft personnel (smoke and survey) and 952 ferry craft including 396 landing craft vehicle personnel and 240 landing craft mechanized, for a total of 2,426 landing ships and craft. These were supported by three battleships, one monitor, 13 cruisers (including one Polish), two gunboats (including one Dutch), 30 destroyers (including two Norwegian), 14 escort destroyers (including two Polish, one Norwegian and one French), four sloops, 42 fleet minesweepers, 87 other minesweepers and danlayers, 19 frigates (including two French), 17 corvettes (including two Greek), 21 anti-submarine trawlers, two minelayers, 90 coastal craft (including 30 American), one seaplane carrier and, to mark the approach lane, two midget submarines.

In reserve Ramsay held one battleship and 40 minesweepers, while the British home commands contributed 20 destroyers (including four American and two Polish), six escort destroyers, 10 sloops, 32 frigates, 50 corvettes (including three Norwegian and one French), 30 anti-submarine trawlers, two minelayers, 292 coastal craft (including 13 Dutch, eight French and three Norwegian) and 58 anti-submarine vessels. The total strength for the whole Allied armada was thus 4,126 landing ships and craft together with 1,213 warships.

The naval arrangements included five Bombarding Forces and five Assault Forces, one of each type being allocated to each of the assault beaches. For the support of the British 3rd Infantry Division's landing on Sword Beach there were Bombarding Force D and Assault Force S commanded respectively by Rear Admiral W.R. Patterson and Rear Admiral A.G. Talbot flying their flags in the cruiser *Mauritius* and command

Above: **The plot-board at Southwick House, the SHAEF HQ near Portsmouth in England, showing the invasion force approaching the beaches.**

Below: **Allied warships tasked with the naval bombardment of the German targets in Sword and British 6th Airborne sectors of the Normandy landings.**

ship *Largs* respectively. Bombarding Force D comprised two battleships, one monitor, five cruisers (including one Polish) and 13 destroyers (including one Norwegian and two Polish). Assault Force S was divided into Assault Groups S3, S2 and S1 carrying the 8th, 185th and 9th Infantry Brigades respectively.

As the ships of Assault Force S approached the Normandy coast, the warships of Bombarding Force D moved ahead of them and followed a van force of minesweepers toward their allotted anchorages off the mouth of the River Orne. The three ships with 15-in guns anchored farthest offshore and opened fire shortly before 0530 hours: the *Warspite* fired at the Villerville battery at a range of some 30,000 yards while the *Ramillies* and the monitor *Roberts* tackled the batteries at Bénerville and Houlgate. The cruisers moved closer inshore and fired on the targets indicated in the map, while the lighter vessels (destroyers and support landing craft) prepared to tackle multiple beach-head targets.

At this point the Germans made their sole naval intervention, when three S-boats sortied from le Havre and fired a salvo of torpedoes, one of which sank the Norwegian destroyer *Svenner*.

Most of the batteries were silenced at least temporarily, and Assault Force S moved into position for the despatch of the landing craft taking the 8th Infantry Brigade to Sword Beach. This was not the end of the naval support operation, which continued through the day as additional ground forces arrived and a number of German batteries showed signs of renewed life that was promptly extinguished by naval heavy guns controlled by orbiting aircraft and, at a later time, radio-equipped shore teams.

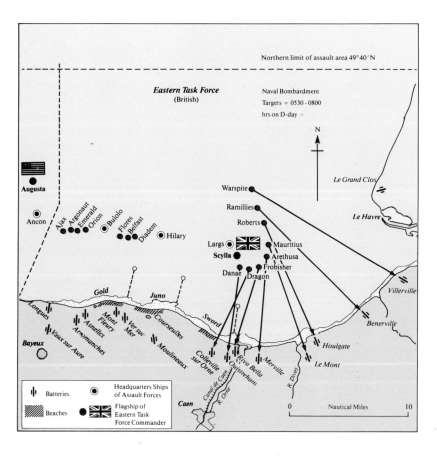